D1997230

Brigitte Köper
Judith Mader

Brush up B1

English Refresher

Kurs- und Arbeitsbuch

Hueber Verlag

Brush up B1
English Refresher

Kurs- und Arbeitsbuch

Brigitte Köper
Judith Mader

Das Werk und seine Teile sind urheberrechtlich geschützt. Jede Verwertung in anderen als den gesetzlich zugelassenen Fällen bedarf deshalb der vorherigen schriftlichen Einwilligung des Verlags.

Hinweis zu § 52a UrhG: Weder das Werk noch seine Teile dürfen ohne eine solche Einwilligung überspielt, gespeichert und in ein Netzwerk eingespielt werden. Dies gilt auch für Intranets von Firmen, Schulen und sonstigen Bildungseinrichtungen.

Eingetragene Warenzeichen oder Marken sind Eigentum des jeweiligen Zeichen- bzw. Markeninhabers, auch dann, wenn diese nicht gekennzeichnet sind. Es ist jedoch zu beachten, dass weder das Vorhandensein noch das Fehlen derartiger Kennzeichnungen die Rechtslage hinsichtlich dieser gewerblichen Schutzrechte berührt.

3. 2. 1. | Die letzten Ziffern
2017 16 15 14 13 | bezeichnen Zahl und Jahr des Druckes.
Alle Drucke dieser Auflage können, da unverändert, nebeneinander benutzt werden.
1. Auflage
© 2013 Hueber Verlag GmbH & Co. KG, 85737 Ismaning, Deutschland
Umschlaggestaltung: Sieveking · Verlagsservice, München
Umschlagfoto: © F1online/Ojo images
Zeichnungen: Bettina Kumpe, Braunschweig
Layout und Satz: Sieveking · Verlagsservice, München
Druck und Bindung: Himmer AG, Augsburg
Printed in Germany
ISBN 978-3-19-002937-2

Contents

Symbols and features

Listening text on CD (12)

One-minute talk

Communication

USEFUL EXPRESSIONS

I'm not sure, but the text might tell us something about …
Look at the title. I guess the text …
I think the text will be about …

Language

REMEMBER

I agree.
I **don't** agree.
➡ Language overview, 1.1

Functions

MY LANGUAGE BOX

I feel happy when ____________________

For me happiness is when ____________________

Introduction

Dear students,

What makes *Brush up B1* different from other books? This is the question you are probably asking yourself at the beginning of your English course. We are sure that you will soon see what is different about *Brush Up B1*, but before you start, take a bit of time to read this introduction.

Do you want to practice speaking and writing English – for your work or for personal reasons? Did you learn English at school or in a course or have you been to England or the USA? Have you forgotten some of what you learnt or are you nervous about speaking English?

We are sure that when you start using English and working with *Brush up B1*, you will remember what you learnt in the past and learn even more! You will enjoy using English and learn more ways of expressing yourself and communicating with others about things which are important to you.

Brush Up B1 is for learners of English who

- know some English grammar and vocabulary but haven't used English for a long time
- want to use English actively in different situations
- want to speak and write English to communicate at work and at home or on holiday
- need vocabulary on up-to-date topics and for everyday situations
- don't want to spend a lot of time on grammar in class but need grammar to use in speaking and writing

Brush Up B1 has

- 4 modules and 12 units, all on interesting topics
- a CD with lively and interesting recordings
- *Extra Practice* for each unit, to do at home or in class
- a reading text for each module
- lists of useful expressions
- a list of what you can do at the end of each module
- explanations of all the relevant grammar with examples in easy English
- a complete tapescript with all the texts of the recordings and a key
- a word list for each unit and an alphabetical word list

When you work with *Brush Up B1*, you will learn to use what you already know and add to it to improve your English. You will become less nervous and more natural when you speak to others in English – whether in the United Kingdom, the USA or anywhere else in the world!

We hope you enjoy working with *Brush Up B1* and wish you success in achieving your goals!

Brigitte Köper, Judith Mader and the Hueber-Team

You and me 1

A new start
Family & friends
Love and happiness

UNIT 1

A new start

1

a **Look at the picture. What kind of questions would you ask to find out as much as possible about these people? In pairs, make a list of five questions.**

REMEMBER

How many ...? **What** kind of ...?
What's ...? **Where** ...?
Why ...?

➡ Language overview, 5

Tina Gregor

b **Now get together with another pair. Compare your questions and choose five questions out of the ten which the four of you find interesting.**

USEFUL EXPRESSIONS

This question is great!
I really like this question.
I agree. / Me, too.
Don't you think this question might / could be too personal?

c **Read the information about Tina and check whether it answers the questions you chose in 1b.**

Name:	Tina	Born:	Freiburg
Family:	two brothers, two cats	School:	Stuttgart
Job:	works in an office	Lives in:	Hamburg
Hobbies:	music, sports	Favourite book:	Lord of the Rings

d **And you? Complete the sentences in the language box about yourself.**

MY LANGUAGE BOX

My name's ___________
I was born in ___________
I've got ___ brothers and ___ sisters.
I work for ___________
I went to school in ___________
I live in ___________
I work in ___________
I'm responsible for ___________

e **Now interview your partner and find out similar information about him / her. Use the questions in 1b. Write down the most important information on a piece of paper. Just write the key words. Then draw a picture of your partner.**

REMEMBER

Where **do you live**?
I live in Hamburg.
This **is** Tina. She live**s** in Hamburg.
She work**s** in an office.

➡ Language overview, 1.1

f **Now take turns to show your picture to the class and present your partner. The key words will help you.**

- This is Tina. She lives in Hamburg with her two cats. …

g **What was the most interesting piece of information you heard?**

- I think the most interesting information is the fact that …

2

a Listen to three people introducing themselves in class. Match the nationalities with the names.

German | Hungarian | Indian

1. Monika ____________

2. Madhu ____________

3. Sebastian ____________

b Listen again. Which languages do they speak?

Monika ______________________________ Sebastian ______________________________

Madhu ____

c Why do Monika, Madhu and Sebastian want to brush up their English? Who says what? Fill in the names.

1. ______________ My daughter is planning to go to California for a year as an au pair, and all the application forms are in English.
2. ______________ So I think I'd like to start work again, and brushing up my English gives me a good feeling for a fresh start in my job.
3. ______________ I feel a bit shy when it comes to speaking English.

d Here are some sentences from the recording. Fill in the missing verbs. Then compare your answers with a partner, listen again and check.

1. I *was*__________ born in Hungary, and when I __________ to kindergarten I learnt to speak German.
2. So it _______ clear that I _______ to learn English.
3. I learnt Spanish quickly because I __________ a lot of friends in Barcelona.
4. After a few years we __________ again, and now I ____________________ in Berlin for twenty years.
5. I __________ an engineer now. Well, to be honest, I __________ a bit shy when it comes to speaking English.

REMEMBER

I was born in …
I went to school in …

I have been living in … for … years.
I have been working for … since …

➡ Language overview, 1.3, 1.5

am | ~~was~~ | had | became | went | feel | moved | needed | have been living

e Why are you brushing up your English? What are your aims?

- At the end of the course I want to speak more fluently.

f What are your partner's aims? Are they the same? What aims do most people in the class have?

3

a Look at the picture. Make a similar word wheel on the board. Add what you think of when you hear the word *au pair*.

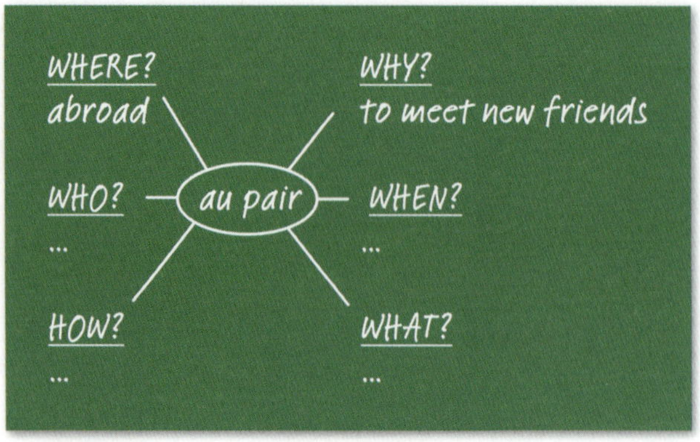

b Have you ever worked as an au pair? Do you know anyone who has done this? Or do you know a family who has an au pair?

c The following article is about *au pair grandmas*. With your partner, discuss why women over fifty might want to go to a foreign country and look after someone else's kids.

d Now read the text and check if your guess was right.

AU PAIR GRANDMAS ARE DISCOVERING THE WORLD

More than 500 women over fifty years of age are registered at *Granny Aupair*, waiting to work in host families. They only need independence and an interest in foreign cultures.

Women of "grandmother age" are in demand. "Au pair grandmas are reliable and bring life experience to the family," says Michaela Hansen, who started *Granny Aupair* agency in 2010. She now has so many inquiries that she has four employees.

The *Granny Aupair* profile: Women over fifty who are interested in travel but don't have enough money for their dream trips. "More than 500 women are registered with us," says Hansen. "There are, of course, favourite places: English-language countries, big cities like New York or London, and of course the typical holiday regions. Some want to go as far as possible, to China or Cambodia, while others prefer to stay near home."

Anke Vendt, sixty-two, from Hamburg was one of the first au pair grandmas. "My two grandchildren are thirteen and eighteen and don't need me as much," she explains. "I applied for a position in Canada, but when Michaela asked me if I would go to Andalusia I said yes. I got a wonderful long holiday that way." She went to a German family living in Spain. They invited her to meet them first and she then went back as "grandma" for seven weeks. "The mother of the children went with her husband on business trips in that time. The two kids, seventeen and thirteen, didn't need bedtime stories, but there was no public transport so I took them to school and picked them up every day. I did the shopping and learned Spanish. The chemistry was good from the very start," says Anke. She had a big room of her own and her room and board were free. Temporary grandmas have gone to many countries, such as the United States, Canada and Africa. They get to know the country and people better than on a holiday.

Michaela Hansen had her own plans to be an au pair when she was younger, but she married at nineteen and had her two kids at twenty and twenty-one. "I thought to myself that there must be other women like me, who still feel young and adventurous." And so the idea was born. Michaela Hansen still hasn't made her original au pair travel plans a reality, but she says "I am so busy now that I don't have time to go anywhere!"

e What is the meaning of the underlined words? Match them with the definitions.

1. They need <u>independence</u>. ☐
2. Au pair grandmas are <u>in demand</u>. ☐
3. They are <u>reliable</u>. ☐
4. Ms Hansen has many <u>inquiries</u>. ☐
5. Her room and <u>board</u> were free. ☐

a. A lot of people would like to have an au pair grandma.

b. Many people are interested and want to know more.

c. She didn't have to pay for her meals.

d. They should be free to travel.

e. You can be sure they care about their job.

f What qualities do au pair employers expect from au pair grandmas? Work with a partner and make a list. Take examples from the text and add your own ideas.

- They have to be reliable. …

g What do you think au pair grandmas expect from their workplace?

- Nice people. …

4

a What would you rather be – an au pair, or someone who is looking for an au pair? Choose your role.

b Michaela Hansen has arranged a video conference for au pair applicants, and families who are looking for an au pair. Work in two groups: group 1 = families / group 2 = au pairs. Each group prepares to ask or answer questions in an interview.

	Group 1 (families)	Group 2 (au pairs)
possible questions	Where are you from? How long do you want to stay? When did you …?	How many …? Where do you …? What kind of …?
possible answers	We are a family of … We live in … We are looking for an au pair who … Yes, you need to look after …	I'm from … I retired ... ago. I am available to start my au pair time … I would like to find a family …

c Then find a partner from the other group and hold the interview for the job. If you don't like the job, move on to another person.

- I'm sorry, but …

d Who found an interesting au pair position? Why was it interesting? Report back to the class.

REMEMBER

I look after the children of my au pair family.
I'm looking for an au pair family in London.
I look forward to hearing from you.

➡ Language overview, 1.16

UNIT 2

Family & friends

1

a Look at the photos and the information that each of these people gives in a social network on the Internet.

Name:	Olivia Cameron	Position:	Assistant Head of Marketing
Gender:	female	Interests:	music, reading, cooking
Date of Birth:	7 th December, 1975	Email Address:	ocamer.nevra@blt.com

Name:	Robert Jutson	Family and friends:	650
Status:	single	Books:	City Boy, Discworld series
Hometown:	Frankfurt	Film:	Braveheart
Languages:	German, English, Spanish, French	Sports:	football, tennis

Name:	Paul Maria Hain	Earlier position:	University Professor
Position:	retired / freelance	Telephone Number:	09876 43567
Status:	married	Contacts:	23

b Use your notebook and put the information into two groups. Compare with a partner. Can you think of any other information?

Personal information	*Interests*

c What information about yourself do you put on the Internet? Discuss with a partner.

d Your English course wants to set up a page on a social network. What information will you ask for: real name / nickname, marital status, favourite restaurant …? Discuss this with the whole class.

USEFUL EXPRESSIONS

I'm married / divorced / single.
seeing someone.
I like films / love stories / thrillers.
going to the … / eating … food.

e In groups, write your profile for the page. What is the name of your class on the social network?

REMEMBER

I like **eating** Chinese food
going to the cinema.

➡ Language overview, 1.15

f Compare all the profiles. Which is the most interesting?

2

a **Draw a table like this one in your notebook and write more words that are connected with families.**

REMEMBER

grandfather | stepmother
mother-in-law | boyfriend
nephew | niece

➡ Language overview, 6.1

people	places	descriptions	feelings
mother	home	large	happy

b **What is a patchwork family? Read the first part of the blog and answer the questions. Discuss your answers with a partner.**

did you know?

Patchwork is used to make new things, such as bedcovers, out of parts of old things, like old clothes. These new things can be really attractive and very valuable. In the same way, patchwork families can also be very happy.

1. Have you ever seen patchwork?
2. Do you do patchwork?
3. Do you know anyone who does it?

c **Now read the next part and talk about the questions with others in your class.**

did you know?

50% of marriages end in divorce and many people with children find a new partner who also has children. These parents and their children are the parts of patchwork families. They sometimes have difficulties at the beginning, because the new partner and the children do not always get on well. But children do not always just lose a parent, they often get a new family member who they also like and respect.

1. Do you agree? Tick.
   Patchwork families …
   - ☐ can be very happy.
   - ☐ find things difficult at the beginning.
2. Do you know any patchwork families?
   What is your experience?
3. Do you know any celebrities who have a patchwork family?

REMEMBER

I agree.
I **don't** agree.

➡ Language overview, 1.1

USEFUL EXPRESSIONS

Camilla is Charles' second wife.
Harry is Camilla's stepson.
… is my father's partner.
… is my stepmother.

3

a **There are more words than just *friend* in English for people you know. How many different words do you know? What are the differences in meaning?**

b **In pairs, match the words to the definitions.**

~~acquaintance~~ | buddy | chum | classmate | companion | pal | partner

1. someone you know and who you see sometimes acquaintance
2. someone you spend a large part of your life with ______
3. three different informal words for *friend* ______
4. someone in the same class as you ______
5. someone you are close to ______

c **How many words are there for *friend* in your language? Do they all mean the same? Look in an online thesaurus for more words in English or your own language.**

3

d **The word *friend* has taken on a new meaning with social network sites. Radio TODAY interviewed people in the street to find out why Facebook is so successful. Listen to what these people think and match the statements to the speakers.**

Speaker 1	Facebook is not for everybody.
Speaker 2	Facebook is a great business idea.
Speaker 3	People like to know what their friends are doing.
Speaker 4	People only join Facebook because their friends do.

e **What is your opinion? Write a statement on a card. Walk around and find out how many people agree or disagree with your statement, then report back to the class. Which statement do most people agree or disagree with?**

USEFUL EXPRESSIONS

I can understand that … but on the other hand …
My opinion of social networks is that they are …
I can't tell you why …
I (firmly) believe …
In my opinion …
I suppose …
I think …

REMEMBER

Don't confuse *I think* and *I mean*.

I think = I have an opinion
I think Facebook is a good way of keeping in touch with friends.

I mean = I can give you more information
I mean, you can communicate so easily with your friends on Facebook.

➡ Language overview, 1.18

f **Here are some tips for using a social network. Do you agree? Write down three more tips in your notebook.**

1. Think before you write.
2. Choose your status carefully.
3. Choose your friends carefully.
4. Make sure you choose the right photo.

g **In pairs, write down three or four statements about a social network like Facebook. Write positive and negative statements. Then change partners and say whether you agree with the statements or not.**

You only need Facebook if you are lonely.
Facebook is a great way to keep in touch with friends.

USEFUL EXPRESSIONS
I absolutely agree with you.
I think the same.
I think so too.
I share your opinion.
I see your point, but …
I'm not sure I agree.

4

a **Read the text about Ronny. Write some information about him in your notebook.**

Age	Nationality	Family	Job

WE WILL NEVER BOMB YOUR COUNTRY

This is a true story. Ronny, a 41-year-old Israeli was fed up with the escalation of hatred between his country, Israel, and Iran, which was triggered by politicians on both sides. So he decided to do something on Facebook which makes sense. He told the Iranian people on his Facebook page that he loved them. Ronny is a father and a graphic designer. He designed his message in a happy, innocent way with nice colours and hearts. His message was: „Iranians, we will never bomb your country, we love you!"

On the same day, about 40,000 Israelis put their families' happy smiles on the Internet. More than fifty-six million people clicked the site. People wrote songs about their sympathy for the Iranians. Iranians put a peace message with music to the Israelis on the Internet. Two new pages appeared: Israellovesiran.com and Iranlovesisrael.com. Politicians had a problem.

People use social networks like Facebook, Twitter, and many others for peace. What happens? No one wants war and no one goes to war. People want to live and let live.

During the Vietnam War in the 1960s there was a slogan: "Imagine there is a war and no one shows up".

b **Answer the following questions.**

1. What did Ronny do?
2. What happened next? What did Iranians / Israelis do?
3. What do you think about what Ronny did?

c **What do people in your class use social networks for? Do a survey.**

to keep in contact with friends	*4*
to share photos with others	…
for business	…

d **Report back to the class. What's the most surprising thing people use social networks for?**

UNIT 2

Love and happiness

1

a **Who are the happiest people in the world? The Spanish? The New Zealanders? The Germans? Discuss this with your partner.**

b **Collect your ideas on the board. Why are these people happy?**

The Spanish
best football team
nice weather

The New Zealanders
beautiful scenery
...

The Germans
...

REMEMBER

nice – nic**er** – nic**est**
beautiful – **more** beautiful – **most** beautiful
good – **better** – **best**
a little – **less** – (the) **least**

The weather in Spain is **better than** the weather in Germany.
The German weather is (not) **as good as** the weather in Spain.

➡ Language overview, 2.1

c **What kind of statements would a really happy person make? In groups, make a short list.**

- I don't want to change anything in my life.

REMEMBER

20%	70%	100%
I slightly agree.	I agree.	I strongly agree.

➡ Language overview, 2.2

d **This is a questionnaire which is used to find out how happy people in different countries are. Read and fill in the numbers from 1 to 7.**

Read the statements below.
Do you agree or disagree?
Use the numbers 1–7.

1 = strongly disagree
2 = disagree
3 = slightly disagree
4 = neither agree nor disagree
5 = slightly agree
6 = agree
7 = strongly agree

__ In most ways my life is ideal or almost ideal.
__ The conditions of my life are excellent.
__ I am satisfied with my life.
__ I have the most important things I want in life.
__ If I could live my life again, I would change almost nothing.

e **Compare the statements in the questionnaire with the statements you've written in c. Are they the same?**

2

a Read about the happiest people in the world. Which country is the article about?

THE HAPPIEST PEOPLE IN THE WORLD

People from ? are the happiest people in the world – again! Followed by Finland, Norway, and the Netherlands, they think that they are very happy. And they expect to lead a happy life in the near future as well. People who took part in the study reported fewer health problems, less stress and sadness, and more happiness, respect and enjoyment. The Gallup study looked at 124 countries, and it's a European country taking the top spot.

b Match a beginning and an ending to make sentences.

1. I heard they have some of the most … d
2. The fish dishes are probably better … ☐
3. The summers in Denmark must be …. ☐
4. I suppose swimming in the North Sea is not as … ☐
5. Do you think football in Denmark is as popular … ☐

a. … colder than our summers.
b. … as it is here?
c. … pleasant as swimming in the Caribbean.
d. … beautiful beaches in Denmark.
e. … than the ones we have in our country.

c Read about Denmark. Would you like to live there? Or in another country? Or would you rather stay where you are? Make a choice. Then get together with the other students who made the same choice.

did you know?

Most people have a job in Denmark. Everyone can read and write. More than half of all school-leavers go on to study at university and education is free. And there is more than just statistics. Denmark has excellent restaurants and even the cafés are better than in many European countries. Copenhagen is one of the most beautiful cities in the world and nowhere in Denmark is more than one hour from the sea where there are beautiful beaches. However, there is one disadvantage. Denmark is more expensive than many countries. But not more expensive than the UK. And the public transport system is better! If you like cycling, hiking, riding, canoeing, windsurfing and sailing, Denmark is the place for your next holiday!

d Each group now makes a list of the advantages of living in the country they chose.

The Danish have a better social security system.
In Germany / Austria / Switzerland we have a wider variety of landscapes, such as high mountains, lakes, and forests.

e Now get together in groups of four (two from each group) and discuss your lists.

f Where do most people in your class want to live?

USEFUL EXPRESSIONS

	agreeing	*disagreeing*
I think Copenhagen is great.	So do I. Me too.	Well, I don't.
I don't think I could live there.	Neither do I. Me neither.	Well, I do.

3

a What makes you happy? Fill in your own ideas and compare with a partner.

L
O
V *anilla ice-cream*
E
H
A
P
P
the f i *rst crocus in spring*
N
E
S
S

b And you? Complete the sentences in the language box about yourself.

MY LANGUAGE BOX

I feel happy when ______________________

For me happiness is when ______________________

It makes me happy to see / hear / feel / watch ______________________

c Was happiness different when you were a child? Talk to your partner.

- When I was a child I loved eating noodles with ketchup. I was really happy when we went camping because then I got my favourite meal every day.

REMEMBER

When I was a child …
I **loved to go** to kindergarten.
I **loved going** to kindergarten.

➔ Language overview, 1.15

d Compare with the rest of the class. What was the funniest reason for feeling happy?

4

a What is a love padlock? Guess.

1. A magic drink that makes your sweetheart love you
2. A lock you hang on a bridge as a symbol for everlasting love
3. A curl from your lover's hair
4. A place where lovers live

b Now read this article and find out if your guess was right.

Locked in love

Have you ever noticed those locks on bridges and wondered what they mean? Just have a closer look and you will find names on them, such as Kathy and Paul, Alicia and Raffaelo, ... Yes, you're right, it has to do with love and happiness. Love padlocks have existed for quite some time, and in Europe they started appearing shortly after the bestseller *I Want You* by Italian author Federico Moccia was published. The main characters in this book swear eternal love, hang a lock with their names on a bridge and throw the key into the river.
You can now see love padlocks all over the world. Famous places are the Hohenzollern Bridge in Cologne, the Brooklyn Bridge in New York, the Most Ljubavi in Serbia, or a lamp post on a bridge in Rome where the locks had to be removed. The bridge was in danger of collapsing – because of the weight of thousands of love padlocks!

c Would you fix a love padlock to a bridge? Do you know someone who has?

5 **d Now listen to an interview on Radio Starlight. Where do Eri, Juan, and Sabrina come from?**

Eri ______ Juan ______ Sabrina ______

5 **e Listen again and fill in the table. Use your notebook.**

	What made them happy when they were children?	What's their tip for being happy?
Eri Juan Sabrina	...	...

f What's your personal tip for being happy? Write down one or two tips on a blank card, then walk around and find someone who has the same tip(s). Which is the best tip for everyone in your class?

UNIT 3

EXTRA PRACTICE UNIT 1

1 This is Eva's story. Read the story and then find the questions.

Story of my life

Hi there! My name's Eva. I was born on a farm in a little village near Passau, and I have got three brothers and two sisters. When I was a child I was responsible for our rabbits, and I just loved playing with them. I went to school in Passau, and when I got a job as a kindergarten teacher I moved to Regensburg. I worked for the local adventure playground, and I really loved my job. And then – something very strange happened to me.

1. was / Where / born? / Eva
   Where was Eva born?
2. brothers / sisters / many / How / has / got? / and / she
   ___
3. pets / kind of / did / have? / she / What
   ___
4. go / Where / did / to / school? / she
   ___
5. was / job? / her / What
   ___

2 Match questions 1–5 to the answers a–e.

3 a. She had rabbits.
_ b. She went to school in Passau.
_ c. Eva was born in a little village near Passau.
_ d. She has got three brothers and two sisters.
_ e. She was a kindergarten teacher.

3a What else would you like to know about Eva? Make questions.

1. Have you got any children? (have got)
2. Where ___ you ___ now? (live)
3. ___ you still ___ as a kindergarten teacher? (work)
4. What ___ the strangest thing that happened to you? (be)

3b What else would you like to ask Eva? Think of more questions.

___

___

4a Now read on and find out what changed Eva's life.

Story of my life

Well, as I said before, something really strange happened to me ... We had a Christmas party for the kids in the kindergarten, and we also invited a Santa Claus to give little presents to the kids. This Santa Claus turned out to be a very nice and attractive man called Thomas. He told me about his life as a teacher in primary school – at the North Cape! Imagine! I fell in love with a man who lives at the North Cape! So now we live in Norway, I work as a kindergarten teacher there, and in my free time – especially in the long winters – I knit pullovers for the tourists who want a souvenir from the North Cape. We've got a little daughter now, her name's Norah. And guess what kind of pets she's got!

4b Here are the answers to the questions in 3a. Fill in the gaps. Did you find the answers to your own questions in 3b?

1. We ________ ________ a little daughter now.
2. We ________ in Norway, at the North Cape.
3. Yes, I still ________ as a kindergarten teacher.
4. The strangest thing that ever happened to me is that I ________ in love with a Santa Claus from the North Cape!

5 Put the words in the correct column. Some can go in more than one column.

course | favourite film | school | actor | application form | ~~engineer~~ | customers | family | making phone calls | adventurous | agency | driving licence | holiday | play the guitar | au pair | travel | favourite place | employees | reliable | brush up my English | office

personal information	job / professional life	learning English
	engineer	

6 Choose two words and use them in one sentence. Bring along your sentences to class. Who has got the funniest sentence?

My family hated it when I learnt to play the guitar.

7 Do you know someone with a surprising life story like Eva's? Write a short story about this person and bring it to class. Try and include two of the words from 5 in your story.

EXTRA PRACTICE UNIT 2

1 Complete the words in the word wheels. Then add one more word to each wheel.

- f _ m _ ly: gr _ ndm _ th _ r, n _ _ ce
- st _ t _ s: m _ rr _ _ d, d _ v _ rc _ d
- p _ s _ t _ _ n: m _ n _ g _ r, w _ _ tr _ ss
- l _ k _ s: r _ _ d _ ng, c _ _ k _ ng
- n _ t _ _ n _ l _ ty: _ ngl _ sh, Fr _ nch
- f _ _ l _ ngs: _ xc _ t _ d, w _ rr _ _ d

2a Lisa lives in Katherine in Australia, a small town of 6,000 inhabitants. A few days ago she listened to an interview on radio TODAY which she found quite interesting. Listen and fill in the gaps.

4

Speaker 1: You ________ ________ ________ who's going out with who …

Speaker 2: Well, people ________ ________ they are connected …

Speaker 3: It's not only ________ ________ so many people use Facebook …

Speaker 4: Facebook is fine ________ ________ ________ ________ thirty-five, but that's it, ______ ______ ________

2b Read about Lisa's life and fill in the words.

live | boring | playing | works | feels | walking | ~~happy~~ | joining | meets | divorced | having | going to

Lisa is quite *happy* with her life in Katherine. She ________ in the local supermarket and ________ a lot of tourists who are on their way to Kakadu National Park. However, she's ________ now, she's forty-four, the kids are out of the house and ________ their own lives, and despite the fact that she likes ________ the Diggers Tavern for a beer with her friend, Janine, she sometimes ________ it's a bit ________ in her small town, and it would be nice to have a few more friends. She enjoys ________ a good conversation, barbecues and picnics, ________ tennis in the cool evening hours, and ________ with her dog, T-Bone. She is toying with the idea of ________ Facebook.

2c Lisa discusses the idea of joining Facebook with her friend, Janine. Read their conversation and match the sentences.

Lisa

1. What do you think? Should I join Facebook? I'd like to make new friends.
2. Do you really believe that? What about Paul? He met his new wife on Facebook – and he's seventy-two!
3. Well, I'm not sure. Anyway, I'm not looking for Prince Charming. I'd just like to chat with a few people.
4. Would you help me set up a profile? I don't know what to write ...

Janine

a. Sure I will. Maybe you'll find some people near here ...

b. I see your point. Why not try it out?

c. Facebook? Well ... I'm not sure. I thought Facebook was only for young people.

d. I guess he's the exception to the rule, isn't he?

3 A few weeks later Lisa and Janine meet the locals at the Diggers Tavern in Katherine. They have just returned from the Todd River Regatta in Alice Springs where they met their new friends from Facebook. Of course everybody wants to know what the meeting was like. Find the questions.

1. do / What / did / you / Alice Springs? / in

   ____

2. story / this / What's / regatta? / the / about

   ____

3. know / Did / each / through / other / Facebook? / everybody

   ____

4. you / What / talk / about? / did

   ____

4 Lisa and Janine brought along a brochure to the pub. Read the story and guess the answers to the questions above.

The Todd River Reggata has been held in Alice Springs every year since 1961. The ironic regatta is held on the dry riverbed, and attracts up to 20,000 spectators. Bottomless boats are picked up by the competitors who stand in them and run down the dry river bed. The regatta was only cancelled once, in 1993, due to flooding – the river had too much water for the race.

5 Now write the answers to the questions in 3 and bring them along to your next lesson. Compare your answers with the others. Are they all the same?

EXTRA PRACTICE UNIT 3

1 Find eight words from the unit.

scenerybeachesprobablyhealthlandscapepadlocksweetheartslightly

2 Underline the odd one out in each group and write down why.

1. tree / rose / hamster / potato / tulip

   A hamster is an animal, all the others are plants.

2. Spanish / German / British / Italy / Danish

   ____

3. happy / beautiful / funny / enjoy / pleasant

   ____

4. read / cycle / write / sail / lake

   ____

5. mountain / lake / see / river / forest

   ____

6. watching TV / riding / canoeing / sailing / hiking

   ____

6 **3** Listen again to Juan (Page 19) and fill in the gaps.

1. Hi there! I'm Juan from Mexico, and in my childhood the __________ moments were – my birthdays!
2. I loved the presents, I loved the parties – and I was allowed to eat ____________________ I wanted! That was great.
3. Now I have a family of my own, and my tip for you is: meet your friends and family _______________ can. You are never __________ than when you're loved!

4 Fill in the table with the correct forms.

	adjective	comparative	superlative
1.			happiest
2.		better	
3.	beautiful		
4.			biggest
5.	expensive		

5 Fill in the gaps.

1. I think that living in Denmark is *more* *expensive* *than* (expensive) living in Germany.
2. I don't think the mountains in Switzerland are ________ ________ (high) the mountains in Germany.
3. I think the Alps are ________ ________________ ________ (impressive) the Himalayas.
4. I guess the ____________ (happy) day in most people's lives is their wedding day.
5. I don't think Australia is ________ ________________ ________ (beautiful) Canada.
6. I guess life in a warm country is much ____________ ________ (cheap) life in a cold climate.

6 Make two more sentences using the words from the table in 4.

I think Copenhagen's football team is not as good as Munich's.
I don't think that Indian elephants are bigger than African elephants.

____

____

7 Look at the statements in 5 and 6 again. Do you agree?

I think that living in Denmark …	*So do I. / Me, too.*	*Well, I don't.*
I don't think the mountains …	*Neither do I. / Me neither.*	*Well, I do.*
I think the Alps …		
I guess the …		
I don't think Australia …		
I guess life …		
I think Copenhagen's …		
I don't think that Indian …		

8 Juan sends an email to a friend in the United States. Underline the correct option.

Dear Maria,
How are you? I hope you're fine and looking *after / forward to* Christmas!
I *visited / visiting* a business partner in Denmark last week, and he invited me *for / at* dinner. Now guess where? A Mexican restaurant! It was *great / really* funny to see what the Danish think is Mexican food. The tortilla was *sweeter / more sweet* than our Christmas cake, and the chilli con carne didn't *had / have* a single chilli! But the wine was as delicious *than / as* our wine at home – thank goodness!
See you soon
Love,
Juan

𝄞♩♪ WE'LL MEET AGAIN, DON'T KNOW WHERE, DON'T KNOW WHEN ... 𝄞♩♪

These are words taken from a song which was popular in the 1940s in Britain. It is from the times when it was much more difficult to keep in touch with friends. There was no email and most people did not even have telephones! Nowadays it is so easy to find people in the Internet and on social networks, so reunions are becoming very popular – of school friends from kindergarten, junior and secondary school, university, college, companies and neighbourhoods. But do we really want to see all these people – old pals and old enemies – again? Sharon Hunter shares her thoughts (and worries) about reunions with us. Sharon is a school teacher. She went to four different schools when she was young and is now a full-time mother of three. She worked in three different schools after she left university before her first child was born.

"I get an invitation to a reunion about every six months now. And I sometimes think 'Do I really want to meet all these people from my past?' I'm not sure. If I want to see them, I can do it without a reunion. I don't think I want to see all the people I have known in my whole life, but maybe there are old friends, acquaintances or colleagues who can become new friends. I've had lots of different experiences at reunions.

I met one of my first bosses at a company reunion and he still made me feel nervous. I always feel like a small child when I see my teachers from school again and don't think I can drink alcohol when they are in the same room! And does my old neighbour remember that I never returned the egg I borrowed from her ten years ago? What about the old classmate who always kicked me under the table when I sat next to her at school? I hated her then but maybe she has changed. I don't think a woman of thirty-eight usually kicks people who sit next to her.

I also worry that no one will know who I am – the last time they saw me was twenty, twenty-five, or thirty years ago. Is my hair too grey? Am I too wrinkled? Am I fat? Everyone else seems to look so young. What do I do if I see an old boyfriend? Did I miss a chance perhaps?

I don't know if the other people at the reunion think I am boring or interesting. Are they still my friends? What happens if we have nothing to say? Maybe their ideas are completely different to mine. Maybe they are richer and have bigger cars. There are so many things to worry about.

An aunt told me that as you get older, you worry less about what people think of you. You keep old friends who are important to you and you make new friends. Even your old boss can become a chum because he is not your boss now. An old teacher can be a friend because you are both adults – and in my case, even colleagues of a sort. All the people you see again at reunions have changed and they can become your new friends. That's something to think about.

So every time an invitation to a reunion arrives in my email box, I feel excited and can't wait to see my old friends (and enemies) again and make them my new buddies!"

About me and my work

My name's …
I was born in …
I have been living in … for …
I'm married / divorced / single.
I'm seeing someone.
I like / love going to the cinema / eating … food.
I feel happy when …
When I was a child I …
I work for …
I'm responsible for …
I retired in …

My plans

I am planning to …
My aims are to …
I'd like to start …
At the end of the course, I want to …
I'm looking forward to going to …
I would like to …
If I could change something, I would …
I don't want to change anything.
I don't think I could …
It would be nice to have …
I don't know if I should …

Asking for and expressing opinions

Don't you think that …
Do you agree?
What do you think about …?
What's your opinion?
I think …
I firmly believe …
I suppose …
In my opinion, …
I can't tell you why …
I can understand that …
On the other hand, …
I absolutely agree.
I think the same.
I'm not sure I agree.
I guess …
Why not …?
I'm not sure.

My useful expression corner

USEFUL EXPRESSIONS

I feel a bit shy / nervous about …
I thought to myself …
I am available to …
I am fed up with …
I am satisfied with …
I can't wait to …

Add some other useful expressions from Module 1 that you want to remember.

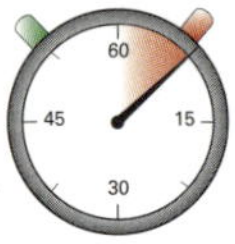

Look back at what you have done in Module 1 and prepare a one-minute talk about social networks. Talk about your experiences with social networks, your opinions of social networks and the reasons for your opinions.

Read the following checklist and tick a smiley.

Now I can …	🙂	😐	☹
… give personal information about myself.			
… say something about my personality.			
… say how I feel about learning English.			
… explain why I want to brush up my English.			
… ask questions to find out about someone.			
… give details about my family and friends.			
… understand short articles in magazines.			
… give my opinion.			
… agree and disagree with opinions and suggestions.			
… give reasons why something is useful or not.			
… compare different things with each other (e.g. places to live).			
… say what makes me happy and why.			
… talk about my past.			
… give advice and tips.			

Think about the following questions and discuss them with a partner.

What was new for you? What did you remember? What would you like to do better? What was the most difficult thing to learn?

The world around us 2

Money

Crime and punishment

Does it matter?

UNIT 4

Money

1

a **What can you (not) do with money? In groups, think of as many examples as you can.**

What can you do with money?	What can you not do with money?
You can save it. You can lend it.	You can't eat it.

b **And what about you? Add one sentence about yourself in the language box.**

MY LANGUAGE BOX

I save some of my money every month.
I never lend money to friends.

____

c **Complete these sayings about money. You can use each word only once.**

lend | borrow | ~~go~~ | spend | earn | buy

Money makes the world (1) ___go___ round.

Money can't (2) ____________ you love.

Don't (3) ____________ your money, before you (4) ____________ it.

Don't (5) ____________ or (6) ____________ for a happy end.

d **Do you agree with the sayings? Which one do you agree with most? And which do you like least? Discuss them with your partner.**

REMEMBER

to borrow ↔ to lend

➡ Language overview, 6.2

2

7

a **Can you say all these numbers? In pairs, read out the numbers and then listen and repeat. Were you right?**

1,456 1,500,000 26 3.25 43,000 750,000 8.83

REMEMBER

A **decimal point** is like a full stop. 7.45: seven point four five

Thousands are shown by a **comma**. 2,500: two thousand five hundred

➡ Language overview, 3.1

b Write down five numbers and dictate them to your partner. Check what your partner writes down. Are the numbers correct?

c Choose one of the numbers together (from your list or the list in a). Now imagine you have this amount of money (in Euros). What would you buy with it or do with it? Collect your ideas on the board.

- I'd buy …
- I'd go …
- I'd …

d What do these things cost? Discuss the prices with your partner.

a flat in a city — a cup of coffee in a café — a newspaper — a car — a box of ten eggs — a bottle of shampoo

USEFUL EXPRESSIONS

I usually pay …
How much is …?
I think a … costs about € …
The cheapest … is just under …
I don't know what a … costs. I never buy …
A flat in a big city can cost from … to …
For the most expensive … there is no limit.
It depends. A … costs between € … and € …

3

a Where do people keep their money? This question can have a lot of answers. How many can you think of? Write down some answers first and then compare them with the others in the class. What's the favourite place?

REMEMBER

I always keep my money in the bank.
I sometimes keep money in a box in the kitchen.

➜ Language overview, 1.1

b Read this text. Then work in pairs and write a text like this about your class.

PEOPLE LIKE KEEPING THEIR MONEY COOL

Forget about keeping money under the mattress. A new survey has found that large numbers of British people keep their money in their fridges.

The survey showed that thirty-one percent of the people asked like keeping their money cool. They put it in plastic bags or containers and hide it at the back of their fridge, behind the food. Only nine percent choose to sleep on their savings. One in ten put their money in a cake tin and about the same number hide the money somewhere else in their home or garden. Twenty-one per cent put their money in a sock in their wardrobe. Nineteen per cent don't know where to hide money best. The fridge was the favourite place. 2,130 adults from England, Wales and Scotland took part in the survey.

REMEMBER

to **take part** = to do something with others
to **take place** = to happen

➜ Language overview, 1.16

4

a Match the following words about money and banks with their meanings.

1. loan
2. security
3. branch

a. something (i.e. a house or a flat) that you agree to give to the bank if you can't pay the money back
b. an office that represents a big company
c. money you borrow from a bank

b In pairs, read the title of the following article. Then read the statements and guess what the article is about.

1. Bankers drink too much alcohol.
2. Banks are planning to sell expensive wines.
3. Fine wine is a good investment. Banks accept it as security.

c Now read the article and write answers to the questions in your notebook. Make sure you say and write the numbers correctly!

BANKERS LOVE FINE WINE

Banks who lend money will take fine wine as security for the loan.

Banks and companies accept wine, jewels and art in return for lending money. This way, they can make a loan on the same day. Lonemoney, a lending agency with 673 branches, say that not long ago they lent $120,000 in return for 128 bottles of wine. The bottles are worth about $250,000.
A case of 1989 Chateau Petrus (12 bottles) is worth about $38,000 and can get you a loan of $24,000 if you don't want to drink it for another six months, which is the time you have to pay back the money. "We lend up to seventy per cent of the value of the wine and the time to pay it back is about seven months. People are using this type of security more and more as it is quick, easy and there is no extra cost!"

1. How many offices does Lonemoney have?
2. How much can you borrow if you have twelve bottles of a Chateau Petrus?
3. When do you have to pay it back?
4. How much of the value of the wine can you borrow?

d What are the advantages and disadvantages of wine as an investment? With a partner, think of three each.

5

REMEMBER

You **could grow** vegetables in your garden.

➡ Language overview, 1.10

a **Could you live without money? With a partner, discuss what you could get without any money.**

b **Before you listen to one man, Andrew Woodruffe, talking about how he lives with no money, look at these questions. What do you think the answers are?**

1. How does he get food?
2. How does he get vegetables and fruit?
3. How did he get a fridge?
4. How does he travel?

8

c **Now listen to Andrew. Were you right? What other questions would you ask him and his family?**

d **What do you think about the way he lives? Can you imagine doing this? How long? When? Where? Alone or with somebody else? In two groups, make a list of all the pros and all the cons of living without money.**

6

a **Andrew says *Most people have too many things*. Do you agree? How many old letters, shoes, clothes, DVDs do you have? Is this too many?**

b **Is there anything else you have too much or too many of? Why? Write two sentences in your notebook.**

I have too many books. There aren't enough shelves in my flat.

REMEMBER

I have **too many** clothes in my wardrobe.
I have **too much** food in my fridge.

➡ Language overview, 3.2

Rudi has **more clothes than** Judith.
Rolf thinks three pairs of shoes is **enough** but Rosa needs thirty-two.

c **What do you do with things you don't want? Think of everything you can do.**

■ I sell them.
▼ I often give clothes I don't want to my friends.

d **Think of something you don't want. Write an advertisement for it and hang it on the wall.**

REMEMBER

It is big / small. *(size)*
It is blue / white. *(colour)*

➡ Language overview, 6.2

I want to sell / give away / exchange ...
It is in good condition. / It is nearly new.
I only used it once.

e **Find someone in the class who wants it. Answer their questions about it.**

■ I think that it is too expensive.
▼ No, it will work for ten more years.

■ Is it big?
▼ Yes, but I'll bring it to your house.

f **Who made the best buy? Who's the best seller in class?**

UNIT 5

Crime and punishment

1

a Which of these things are wrong? Tick. Which is the most serious? Which is worst? Compare your ideas with a partner.

- ☐ 1. phoning in sick at work when you are not really ill
- ☐ 2. travelling without a ticket on public transport
- ☐ 3. crossing the road when the light is red
- ☐ 4. taking printer paper home from work
- ☐ 5. copying a CD for a friend
- ☐ 6. copying in a class test

b Have you ever done any of them? Interview some people, then report back. Which is the funniest story?

REMEMBER

Have you ever **done / made / been** …
No, **I've** never **done / made / been** …
I've often **done / made / been** …

I **did / made / was** … **last year / yesterday**.

➔ Language overview, 1.4, 1.3

c Match these words to the expressions in a.

doing a sickie (_1_) fare-dodging (__)

stealing (__) cheating (__)

jaywalking (__) piracy (__)

REMEMBER

Travel**ling** without a ticket is wrong.
Cross**ing** the road when the light is red is okay.

➔ Language overview, 1.15

MY LANGUAGE BOX

I have never cheated in a test.
I always pay for my ticket on public transport.
I would never do a sickie.
I travelled without a ticket last week.

d Did you know? – In Great Britain many people think cheating in tests at school is very bad. It is almost like stealing from your friends. Do you agree?

10

e Laura Smith is a teacher at Arbourne Junior School. She explains to parents what will happen if pupils cheat. Listen and answer the questions.

1. Why do pupils cheat in tests at school?
2. What is the punishment for cheating?

2

a What do you think about these things? Are they against the law? Are they right or wrong? Discuss with your partner.

1. using a shopping trolley for transporting your things home
2. washing your car on Sunday
3. playing the piano at midday

b Read and fill in the gaps. Do you think the judge was right?

catch drink drive ~~have~~ say take think

When I was 18, I *had* (1) to pay a fine of €200 because some friends __________ (2) me home from a pub in a shopping trolley which they __________ (3) from outside a supermarket. I __________ (4) a beer during the ride, and we __________ (5) it was a lot of fun! Unfortunately the police __________ (6) us and the judge __________ (7) it was stealing.

c Which of the examples in (a) are illegal in your country, or in a country you have visited? Have you ever had trouble with the law in a foreign country? Tell the others.

REMEMBER

I had to pay a fine.

➜ Language overview, 1.13

3

REMEMBER

If you mow**ed** the lawn on Sundays, my neighbours **might / would** complain.

➜ Language overview, 1.10

a What would happen in your country / town / area / house? Use your notebook and complete the answers. Then write three more questions and ask your partner.

What would happen if you played loud music at midnight?
What might happen if you mowed the lawn on Sunday?

If I played ...
If I ...

b What should you do? Discuss these questions with your partner.

- What should you do … if you find €100 on the street?
  if a friend wants to drive when he is drunk?
- If I found …

c Think of some more questions like this. Ask another pair. Make a list of answers people in the class give you.

USEFUL EXPRESSIONS

I have a problem. … What should I do?
Let me give you some advice. If you see someone stealing, you should …

4

a **Match the parts of these words. They are all crimes.**

1. hi	a. napping	5. pick	e. bery
2. vanda	b. lifting	6. rob	f. pocketing
3. kid	c. jacking	7. burg	g. ging
4. shop	d. lism	8. mug	h. lary

b **Do you know what the crimes are? Use a dictionary. Can you think of any more? Are they a problem in your town or city?**

USEFUL EXPRESSIONS

I don't know what vandalism is.
What is the difference between … and …?
Pickpocketing is a big problem in cities.

c **What are the people called who commit these crimes? If necessary, use a dictionary to find out.**

1. Someone who kills someone: *a killer*
2. Someone who damages property: ________
3. Someone who takes a person away by force and asks for money to return him or her: ________
4. Someone who takes an aeroplane or ship by force: ________
5. Someone who breaks into a bank and steals money: ________

d **And what do these criminals do? Write the complete sentences in your notebook.**

A shoplifter is someone who …
A mugger …
A burglar …

e **Do you know what these punishments are? Can you think of any more? Are they a good idea? Discuss them in small groups.**

prison
probation
fine
community service

5

a **There are many rules for drivers. What can drivers do wrong? Add two more things.**

They can drive too fast.
They can park in the wrong place.

b **Think of the rules you agree with and don't agree with. Compare with your partner.**

- I think wearing seatbelts is a good idea.
- I don't like speed limits.

c **Should there be a speed limit on motorways? Read the following article.**

SPEED LIMITS

Britain has a speed limit of 70 mph* (about 113 kph**) on motorways which may not seem very high, especially to Germans. In Abu Dhabi, it was 99 mph (160 kph) from 2005 to 2010 but this was reduced to 87 mph (140 kph) recently. This is about the average speed people drive on some parts of Germany's motorways, where there is no speed limit at all. There are a few other places where there are no speed limits, but also perhaps not many cars, like the Isle of Man, a small island off the west coast of England. The Isle of Man is famous for motor racing, so maybe that is the reason!

Most other European countries have speed limits and most are higher than the UK. The highest are in the Czech Republic, Romania and Denmark at 81 mph (130 kph) and the lowest are in Sweden, Latvia and Moldova at 69 mph (110 kph). Belgium, Spain and Switzerland are somewhere in the middle with speed limits of 74 mph (120 kph).

In the United States, there are different speed limits in different states and there are sometimes even different speed limits in one state, like Texas. In Utah, the speed limit is 80 mph (129 kph) and in Hawaii 60 mph (97 kph).

In general, lower speed limits mean fewer accidents so speed limits are becoming lower everywhere, but also less fixed. On many motorways, speed limits change depending on traffic and weather conditions.

* miles per hour ** kilometres per hour

d **Fill in the table with speed limits on motorways for four countries.**

Country				
Speed limit				

e **Think of all the arguments for and against speed limits and have a class debate.**

6

a **Here are some funny laws. They all exist! Can you think of reasons for these laws? Discuss some reasons in groups.**

§ It is illegal to stand around any building without a good reason to be there.

§ Citizens may not enter Wisconsin with a chicken on their head.

§ It is illegal to sell peanuts after the sun goes down on Wednesday.

§ You must not open an umbrella on a street if a horse is near.

§ You may only have one alcoholic drink in front of you at a time.

§ All men driving motorcycles must wear shirts.

b **What will / can / might happen if you break one of these rules?**

c **In small groups, think of three funny rules for your English class. What will happen if you break these rules? Think of three funny punishments. Then report back to the class. Which group has the funniest rule / punishment?**

UNIT 6

Does it matter?

1

a **Vocabulary ping-pong. How many words can you think of? Get together with a partner and brainstorm words for the following categories. Take turns in finding words. After a minute go to the next category.**

apple — fruit — banana
pear

fruit · shops · vegetables · means of transport · animals

11

b **Susan had a strange experience. How does she feel, and why? Listen to her podcast and answer. Compare with a partner.**

c **What else can you guess about Susan's shopping habits? Work with a partner and match the beginnings and endings to make meaningful sentences.**

1. Susan never used to check [c]
2. She used to think that the food in [ ]
3. She never used to buy food from [ ]
4. She used to believe that [ ]
5. Her family never used to grow [ ]

a. the supermarket was locally grown.
b. buying cheap was the most important thing.
c. where the food was grown.
d. vegetables in the garden.
e. local farmers.

d **Write about yourself and your family. Finish the following sentences in your notebook.**

1. When my mother was a child she used to walk to school.
2. When I was a teenager I used to ...
3. Everybody in my family used to ...
4. When I was a child I never used to ...
5. When my grandmother was young she used to ...
6. I used to ... but I don't do it anymore!

REMEMBER

I always **used to** buy things in the supermarket.

➜ Language overview, 1.6

e **Write two sentences about yourself. Walk around and read out your sentences. Try and find others with the same information. How many students have the same sentences?**

MY LANGUAGE BOX

When I was a child / teenager / young father …
When my grandmother was a young girl …

2

12 a **Let's get back to Susan. What do you think happens next? Listen how the story goes on.**

12 b **Listen again. Susan mentions a few reasons why she is angry. Make a list in your notebook and compare with a partner.**

She is furious because …
1. ____________________
2. ____________________

c **Work in groups. Read and answer the questions. Then report back to the class and collect your ideas on the board.**

Think of the food you or your family recently bought.
1. Which products are imported from far away places?
2. Where do these products come from?
3. How are they transported?
4. How much do they cost (compared to local products)?

USEFUL EXPRESSIONS

Lately I was shopping …
I got a flyer the other day …
Two weeks ago I bought …
There was a special offer last week …

d **Susan said she needed to change something. What did she do? Collect a few ideas with your partner and write them on the board.**

food — *buy from local farmers*
costs
transport

3

a **This is the headline of a leaflet Susan found in her letterbox the other day. What do you think it is about?**

Welcome to Freshly Farmed!

b **Here are some words from the leaflet. Match the words and their meanings. Compare with a partner.**

1. increasingly	a. grown without fertilizers, pesticides or genetic manipulation
2. trusted	b. to become a member of the organisation
3. to join	c. to adapt to your own needs
4. nutrient rich	d. full of healthy ingredients
5. organic food	e. more and more
6. to customize	f. reliable

c **Now read the leaflet and answer the questions. Compare with a partner.**

Welcome to Freshly Farmed!

People are becoming increasingly interested in where their food comes from and how it is grown and so are interested in connecting directly to a local farm. *Freshly Farmed* is becoming a popular alternative for getting high quality food from a trusted local source. Customers are connecting directly to a farm nearby.

You can receive regular deliveries of nutrient-rich, mouth-watering organic produce delivered to your home or office.

Our service is customer friendly, flexible, and convenient – cancel any time – no commitment. We deliver directly to your home or office, weekly, every other week or monthly.

Customize your delivery – exclude items you do not like and add extra items you do. Receive deliveries starting at only € 20 per delivery. Satisfaction guaranteed. Speak with friendly customer service Monday to Friday 8.00 am to 5.00 pm.

1. What does *Freshly Farmed* deliver?
2. What are the delivery conditions?

REMEMBER

People **are** becom**ing** increasingly interested in …
Freshly Farmed **is** becom**ing** a popular alternative …
Customers are connect**ing** directly …

➜ Language overview, 1.2

USEFUL EXPRESSIONS

weekly
every other week
monthly
once / twice / three times a month

d **Work in pairs and make a phone call to *Freshly Farmed*.**

Student A is the customer. Make notes on what you want to buy and questions you have.
Student B works for *Freshly Farmed*.
Think about the questions your customer might have.

USEFUL EXPRESSIONS

Hello, this is ... speaking.
Can you ... Would you ...
I'm interested in ...
How much is ...?
I'd like some information on ...
What time ...?

4

a **New ideas on gardening and farming are developing. What do you think is behind these headlines?**

VERTICAL GARDENING

VERTICAL FARMING

b **Read the following articles on the latest trends in gardening and farming and add the headlines from a.**

______________________________ (1)

Patrick Blanc's projects allow plants and buildings to live in harmony with one another. The landscape designer is probably best known for his great living wall on the Musée du Quai Branly in Paris. With Blanc's Vertical Garden System you can grow all sorts of plants indoors and outdoors – in any climate.

______________________________ (2)

This is a concept that argues that it is economically and environmentally viable to cultivate plant or animal life within skyscrapers. The idea of a vertical farm has existed at least since the early 1950s, and the aim is to bring farming back to the consumer. The modern idea of vertical farming uses techniques similar to glass houses, where natural sunlight can be augmented with artificial lighting.

c **Choose either *vertical gardening* or *vertical farming*. Form two groups. In your group, discuss advantages and disadvantages of these ideas.**

d **Susan checked the Internet for a forum where people exchange their ideas on reducing their carbon footprint. Read and match the forum entries and replies. Compare with a partner.**

1 ☐

greenthumb@yahoo.fr Hi there, my name's Rita. I think city gardening is a fantastic idea, and my neighbours are even taking the idea further. They have chickens in their garden – in the city of Marseille! Fresh eggs every day – that's great!

2 ☐

kudamm@gmx.de Hi there, this is Joan. I live in Berlin, and we have a very active guerrilla gardening group here, you know, planting flowers and bushes in all sorts of places in the city without legal permission. The results are fantastic – have a look at these pictures.

a ☐

cheguevara@uk.google.com Hello, I'm Rob and I just had a brainwave: How about guerrilla farming? Big cities like Berlin or New York never have enough space for growing vegetables locally, so why not use the open space in cities for growing tomatoes and pumpkins? Let's have a new group – join me – let's do it!

b ☐

bham38@google.uk Hi, I'm Justin, and sure it's nice to have your own fresh eggs every day – but it's hard for the neighbours! Mine have a rooster which crows at 4.30 a.m. every morning – in the centre of Birmingham! Seven days a week! I'm really desperate!

e **Get together with a partner and write to the forum. You can add to the entries in d, or start a new idea. And of course, you can disagree! Write your entry on a separate piece of paper and hang it on the wall. Which is the funniest? Which is the most interesting? Which group would you join?**

EXTRA PRACTICE UNIT 4

1a Money, money, money! Put the letters in the correct order.

I X P N S E E E V	S U I R E C T Y	R A C B N H	U L E V A	P E C I R	O L N A	A B K N
expensive	______	______	______	______	______	______

1b Fill in the missing vowels and match the beginnings and endings of the sayings.

1. Money can't → b.
2. Don't sp__nd your money
3. Don't b__rr__w or l__nd

a. for a happy end.
b. b__y you love.
c. before you __ __rn it.

1c Unjumble these words.

CEHAP ______ LSEL ______

SCOT ______ PYA ______

1d Find the opposites.

to borrow ↔ ____________

to save ↔ ____________

2a Is it *point* or *comma*? Match the numbers and the words.

1. 1.5 litres of milk → e.
2. € 6,378
3. 42.195 km
4. $ 1,500,000
5. 0.568 m

a. six thousand three hundred and seventy-eight …
b. one million five hundred thousand …
c. forty-two point one nine five …
d. oh point five six eight …
e. one point five …

2b Which of the figures above is the distance of a marathon?

3 Listen to Andrew Woodruffe (Page 33) again and fill in the money words in their correct form.

9

1. They live without ____________ any money.
2. This means they also don't ____________ or ____________ money.
3. And how did you get a freezer and a fridge? They usually ____________ money.
4. Andrew, you don't ____________ money. But do you ____________ money?
5. We live in our own house and we ____________ for electricity and gas and water.

4 Put the words in the correct order. The first card has been marked.

SMO HAN RET THE SAL REI WEN EED. WAY

1. *There is always more than we need.*

OOD HEL LES EVE LYC ANE RYD AY. ATN

2. *Helly*

SMO AFR EUS NEY. UAL LYC OST IDG

3. *A fridge*

END EY. MON WEN RSP EVE ANY

4. *We*

INK MIL K. FTE NDR WEO

5. *We*

5 Is it *much* or *many*? Put the words into the correct basket. Then add three more words to each basket.

~~friends~~ eggs coffee shampoo money fridges flats offices wine clothes

much ____________________

many *friends*

6a *Too much* or *not enough*? Finish the sentence beginnings. Write what is true for you.

1. I have too many ____________________.
2. My friends have more ____________________ than me.
3. There is too much ____________________.
4. Our town has not enough ____________________.
5. I like ____________________ more than ____________________.
6. There are not enough ____________________ in my town.

6b Take your sentences to class and compare them with two other students. Are they all the same?

EXTRA PRACTICE UNIT 5

1 Connect the dominos in the correct order. The first pair has been connected for you. Then write down the correct combinations. Use your notebook.

from a shop	copy in a
at midday	wash your car on
home from work	cheat
Sunday	steal
a ticket	taking printer paper
in a test	do a
class test	travelling without
sickie	play the piano

2 Irregular verbs quiz: What's the missing form? Fill in.

give		
	spent	
		seen
feel		

	was / were	
have		
		done

3a Read Susanne's blog and answer the following questions.

1. Has she ever had problems when travelling?
2. How many years of her life has she spent travelling?
3. Which destination is number one on her wish list?

Travel Chatter

Last year somebody (1) *gave / has given* me the book *1,000 Places To See Before You Die*, and when reading it I was amazed to learn that I (2) *have seen / was seen* a lot of these places myself!

Ever since I was a little girl I (3) *have felt / will feel* wanderlust – probably because I (4) *am / was* born in a remote village in Bavaria! My family (5) *has been / was* not really well off, and my most exciting trips in my childhood were to the Bavarian Forest.

As soon as I was old enough to get a job and earn some money during my summer holidays I (6) *have started / started* saving up to travel. When I was sixteen I made my first trip and travelled through Italy. I only (7) *have / had* about four hundred German marks (200 Euros) for four weeks, so it was backpacking, camping, and bread and tomatoes nearly every day. I didn't mind. I made it to Florence and Rome. I (8) *saw / seen* Naples, and the dolphins swimming in the Mediterranean. I loved it! It was such a great experience!

I have been travelling around the world ever since. I (9) *have done / will do* exotic trips like riding on the Transsiberian Railway, sailing on Pearl River in communist China, and climbing the volcano Mount Bromo on Java on Christmas Eve.

And I have been lucky – I (10) *have never had / will never have* any problems at all! I have never been robbed or mugged, I have never been cheated, and nobody ever threatened or hurt me.

So far I have spent about six years of my life travelling, and I have seen 367 of the places they mention in the book. But there are so many countries and areas I (11) *have not visited / had not visited* yet! Number one on my wish list is Sequoia National Park in Sierra Nevada, California. It must be great to sit under one of those giant sequoia trees and feel what it is like to have lived over 3,000 years! How much could you travel if you lived 3,000 years? Well, not as a tree, of course!

3b Read again and underline the correct form of the verb.

4 Complete the following questions that you could ask another student.

1. *Have you ever worked* (work) during your summer holidays?
2. ______________________ (read) a book about travelling?
3. ______________________ (be) robbed or mugged?
4. ______________________ (feel) wanderlust?
5. ______________________ (travel) to China?
6. ______________________ (see) a crime?
7. ______________________ (be) to Rome?

5 Add some follow-up questions to each question in 4. Use your notebook.

Question 1
When was it? What...

6 Answer the questions yourself. Write down a few sentences about your experiences.

7 Take your questions from 4 and 5 and your own answers from 6 to class and interview another student. Who has the most interesting story?

EXTRA PRACTICE UNIT 6

1 **The following words have been taken from the unit. Can you put them into groups? Choose your own groups. Some words can go in more than one group.**

pineapple ~~garden~~ local ~~farm~~ grow teenager young father believe furious fly car pear shop supermaket buy kiwi healthy think orange organic fresh deliver mouth-watering bike

places	*adjectives*	*what I like*			
garden					
farm					

2 **Now choose two words from different categories and use them in one sentence. Make four sentences with different words.**

They say pineapples are very healthy.

____

____

____

____

3 **Take your sentences to class. How many students have got the same sentences?**

13 **4** **Listen to Susan (Page 38) again and choose the correct option.**

You know, something strange happened to me (1) *late / lately*. I was shopping at the supermarket (2) *usually / as usual*. I bought all sorts of things, and especially a lot of (3) *vegetables / vegetarians* because I wanted to make a ratatouille for my friends, you know, courgettes, aubergines, tomatoes, garlic, the lot. I mean I always (4) *buy / am buying* things in the supermarket, I don't have (5) *many / much* time to go from small shop to small shop, so the supermarket is the most convenient place for my shopping. When I came (6) *at home / home* I unpacked my stuff, and just like that and for no special reason, I glanced at the little label on the garlic, and I (7) *red / read* "Garlic from Argentina". What? Argentina? I just couldn't believe my eyes!

5 **What did you use to do when you were younger? Write about yourself or a friend.**

1. play volleyball – play computer games

   I used to play volleyball, but now I play computer games.

2. spend my holiday in Italy – fly to exotic countries

   ____

3. go skiing – go hiking

4. smoke – eat a lot of cake

5. wear miniskirts – wear trousers

6. buy records – download music from the Internet

7. be poor – be rich

8. buy things in shops – buy online

6 **What other trends have you heard of? Look at the pictures and describe the trends.**

1. *More and more people are buying organic food in the supermarket.*

2. ______

3. ______

4. ______

5. ______

4 people report

HOW I LEARNT TO MANAGE MY MONEY

Debbie, 22, trainee office manager

I never had any money at the end of term when I was a student. I always owed my mates money and had an overdraft at the bank. Often my dad paid it off, but when I finished university, I realised I would have to look after my money better and be independent of my mum and dad. I want to buy a flat and need some cash for that. Strangely enough, the first thing I did to save money was to spend it! I bought a bike and now cycle to work. That way I save loads on underground fares. I did a cookery course and bought recipe books. I never eat out now but cook for myself and for my friends. It's fantastic fun and saves me lots of money! Those are just two examples. Although I spent money at first, in the end I saved more than I spent and can soon start looking for my own home with a bigger kitchen!

Martin, 52, bank manager

I got divorced two years ago and have to pay my ex-wife maintenance as she looks after the children. So although I earn a good salary, my life is much more expensive than it was. I know from my work that people often go into debt and even become bankrupt when they get divorced and didn't want that to happen to me. I moved into a flat but had no idea how to run a household, cook, wash or go shopping as my wife looked after everything when we were married. So I got books out of the library about housekeeping and learnt where to shop for cheap food and how to cook and use the washing machine economically. I spent a lot of time thinking about my money and worked everything out very carefully. It was hard but I did it!

Jennie, 31, housewife and mother

My life changed when my daughter was born. I decided to give up work and stay at home for a long time. I know it seems old-fashioned but we want to have more children and, as a teacher, I can go back to work again after twelve years or so. But it meant a big difference to our financial situation. We decided to cut down on big things. We sold one of our cars, so Paul, my husband, goes to work by bike or by bus. And we go to holiday homes instead of hotels for our holidays. We buy most things second-hand, which we never did before but it's amazing what good stuff you can get!

Leo, 28, shop assistant

I have just started a new job where I earn quite well, but had lots of debts from the time when I was unemployed and went through a difficult period in life. I spent too much and seemed to get bills all the time (like for my mobile, electricity, credit card and so on) and couldn't pay them. They just got bigger and I couldn't sleep for worry. My best friend advised me to ask my mother and she agreed to help me out. I didn't want to tell her because I thought she would worry, but it was the best thing I did. She lent me the money and told me to write down everything I spent so I knew how much I could pay back each month. I am paying her back but she isn't charging me interest so I think I can manage to get into the black again soon.

About money

I earn a good salary.
I never borrow or lend money.
I try to save money every month.
I spend a lot of money on food.
You have to pay about … for a small car.
I never buy wine so I don't know what it costs.
How much do ten eggs cost?
A flat in a big city can cost about …
The cheapest car costs about …
The best place to keep money is in the bank.
There are many ways to invest money well.

Right and wrong

Travelling without a ticket is wrong.
It is not a good idea to cross the road when the lights are red.
What is a good punishment for speeding?
There shouldn't be a speed limit on the motorway.
If you wash your car on a Sunday, people will complain.
It is against the law to drive when you are drunk.
It is illegal to take a trolley from the supermarket.
Vandalism is a big problem nowadays.
A hijacker is someone who takes a plane or ship by force.
I have never cheated in a test.

Talking about the past

I have never ….
Have you ever …?
When was it?
No, I've never done / made / been …
I've often done / made / been …
I did / made / was … last year / yesterday.
I used to … but I don't any more.
Lately I was in the supermarket when …
The other day I saw …
Two weeks ago I …
There was a special offer last week …

Talking about trends

People are becoming increasingly interested in fresh food.
Farm produce is becoming a popular alternative to supermarket food.

My useful expression corner

USEFUL EXPRESSIONS

The wine is worth a lot of money.
I have too many clothes in my wardrobe.
It is in good condition.
It will work for a long time.
What's the difference between … and …?
I was furious because …

Add some other useful expressions from Module 2 that you want to remember.

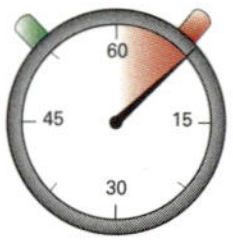

Look back at what you have done in Module 2 and prepare a one-minute talk about money. Talk about how you feel about money, your opinion of living without money and the reasons for your opinions.

Tick a smiley for each item in the list:

Now I can …	☺	😐	☹
… talk about what I do with money.			
… say and write numbers correctly (thousands and decimal points).			
… say what things cost.			
… compare prices of different things.			
… talk about borrowing and lending money.			
… talk about advantages and disadvantages of different investments.			
… ask and answer questions about living without money.			
… say what I do with things I don't want.			
… say if I have ever done something wrong.			
… say how I feel about doing things which are wrong or illegal.			
… describe what would happen if someone did something wrong.			
… talk about things which were different in the past.			
… make a phone call to get information.			

Think about the following questions and discuss them with a partner.

What was new for you? What did you remember? What would you like to do better? What was the most difficult thing to learn?

Changes 3

Global changes
(Dis)Connected?
Unusual hobbies

Global changes

1

a Imagine you need something or you want to explain something but you don't know the word. What can you do? Choose from the following suggestions.

- ☐ You describe it.
- ☐ You try and find examples.
- ☐ You forget about it.
- ☐ You try and define it.

b Read the description and guess what it is.

It's kind of round, white outside, the inside is white and yellow. You can eat it. Many people paint it for Easter. – What is it? It's ____________

c Now work with a partner and guess words. Each of you will get a list of five words. Don't show them to your partner! Explain your words without actually saying them. Your partner will try and find out what the words are.

Student A looks at page 95.
Student B looks at page 96.

USEFUL EXPRESSIONS

It's ... cm high / ... cm long / ... cm wide.
It's made of metal / plastic / wood.
You need it for making ...
You use it to make ...
It's a person who ...
It's a thing which ...
It's kind of a ...

2

a Match the following words with their definitions.

1. tribes
2. territory
3. hunting
4. bows and arrows
5. rainforest
6. crops

a. used for hunting and sport
b. chasing and killing wild animals
c. forest in a tropical region
d. an area of land
e. plants grown for food
f. large groups of related families who live in the same area and share the same language

b Look at the list of words in 2a (marked green). They are all taken from the text you are going to read in c. What do you think the text will tell you? Compare with a partner.

USEFUL EXPRESSIONS

I'm not sure, but the text might tell us something about ...
Look at the title. I guess the text ...
I think the text will be about ...

c Now read the text. Fill in the words from a.

AMAZON TRIBES

The Amazon area is the world's largest (1) ____________. It is also the home of one million Indians. They are divided into about 400 (2) ____________, each with its own language, culture and (3) ____________. Many have had contact with outsiders for almost 500 years. Others – "uncontacted" tribes – have had no contact at all.

They also hunt and fish, using plant-based poisons to kill the fish. Some tribes use shotguns for (4) ____________, others use (5) ____________, spears, or blowguns with darts tipped with poison.

Only a few Amazonian tribes are nomadic; most of them live deep in the forest away from the rivers. They grow some (6) ____________ but rely more on hunting and gathering.

REMEMBER

They **have had** contact with outsiders for almost 500 years.
Others **have had** no contact at all.

➡ Language overview, 1.4

3

a **Find the questions. Write them in your notebook. Leave some space after each question.**

1. person / you / have / met / a / from / ever / an / "exotic" / country?
2. have / you / heard / a / very / ever / unusual / language?
3. you / on / river? / big / have / ever / travelled / a
4. a / you / have / spoken / to / fisherman? / ever
5. have / to / you / been / the / ever / rainforest?
6. you / visited / ever / South / have / America?
7. met / have / hunter? / you / ever / a

Have you ever met a person from an "exotic" country?
Which country was it?
...

REMEMBER

Have you ever **been** to Brazil?
When **was** that?
Have you ever **travelled** on a big river?
Where **did** you **go**?

➡ Language overview, 1.4, 1.3

b **Now match each question in 3a to one of the follow-up questions below. Use your notebook and write a follow-up question next to the appropriate question. There is more than one possible match.**

Which country was it? | Where did you go? | When did you go? | Which language was it? | What did he say? | What was it like? | Where was it?

c **Work in small groups and use the questions from 3a and 3b. Interview each other about your travels. Don't forget to ask a lot of questions to find out something interesting. Report back to the class. What is the most interesting or the funniest story?**

MY LANGUAGE BOX

I have been to the jungle several times. The first time I went by train and ...
I have often travelled on rivers. The last time was in August. I was ...
I have never been to Brazil. But I certainly would like to go! My plan is to ...
No, but I have ...

4

a Look at this wordsnake. Which words can you identify? Compare with a partner.

COOKERSOLARLAMPENERGYELECTRICALPOWERBENEFIT

b What do the words mean? Ask your partner and the teacher. Use the expressions from 1c to describe them.

14

c Laura is an expert on solar energy. Listen to the interview on *Radio Tomorrow* and answer the following questions.

1. What's the topic of this broadcast?
2. Which country are they talking about?
3. How many people in the Amazon area live without electrical power?

14

d Listen again and finish the sentences and compare.

1. In this broadcast we're talking to people who bring ______________ into the world.
2. In the Amazon area? ______________ in Brazil?
3. ______________ does this mean?
4. ______________ they live without lamps, without cookers ...
5. So ______________ that one million people in Brazil live ...
6. Sorry? ______________ Gensets? ______________

e Work in pairs. You are going to read short texts to each other. Some words will be hard to understand. You will have to ask your partner to explain them.

Student A looks at page 95.
Student B looks at page 96.

MY LANGUAGE BOX

Can you repeat that, please?
Sorry? I didn't really get that.
Could you say that again?

15

f What do you think a *genset* is? Listen to the second part of the interview and choose one explanation.

- ☐ A machine used to generate electricity.
- ☐ An international group of rich people.

15

g Read, listen again and underline the correct words. Then compare your answers with a partner.

REMEMBER

this machine
these machines

➜ Language overview, 4.2

radiotomorrow www.radiotomorrow.com

Laura: A genset is a generator powered by *fuel / fully* or gas, and it creates electrical power. You use *these / this* machines in places where you don't *normal / normally* have access to electrical power from the grid. For example, in far-away *islands / Iceland*, or when you build roads or new buildings, you need gensets. And you have emergency gensets in modern hospitals and hotels, just in case of a power shortage.

Interviewer: Okay ... But you said they need fuel? Where does it come from?

Laura: That's a good question. Most Indian tribes *need / meet* a 3-day-trip to get some fuel. First they walk through the jungle to the nearest river, then they paddle their canoes up or down the Amazon to *buy / by* fuel in some small town, and finally they paddle and carry huge cans with fuel back home.

Interviewer: Phew ... that doesn't sound very *convenient / comfortable*.

Laura: No, definitely not.

Interviewer: So what will change now?

Laura: Solar energy is the solution. Modern systems can stand alone wherever they are needed in the world, and they *produce / product* energy without any trouble.

5

a **Think about the changes solar energy will bring to the Amazon Indians. What about their social life, daily routine, education, culture, and so on? Make a list. Then get together with two or three other students and compare. Write your ideas on the board.**

They used to go hunting for fresh meat but soon they will have freezers and eat pizza.

b **Now think about your own life and the way you use energy. What did you do in the past? And what will you do in the future? Work in pairs and write your statements on blank cards.**

c **Give your card(s) to your teacher. Your teacher will give you a different one. Read it out to the class. Can you guess who wrote it?**

I used to take the car to go to work but from now on I will ...
My grandfather used to switch off the lights whenever he left the room but ...

(Dis)Connected?

1

a What's a *black hole resort*? Choose an answer and compare with a partner.

A *black hole resort* is …

- ☐ a dark cave where endangered animals can live in peace and quiet.
- ☐ a hotel resort without TV, mobile phones and Internet access.
- ☐ a galaxy in space where you can find a lot of black holes.

b Read this article on *black hole resorts*. Which paragraph goes best with which headline? Match and compare with a partner.

4 SLOW THINKING IS DEEP THINKING

___ AN EXPENSIVE PRIVILEGE

___ SO WHAT CAN WE DO?

1 WHY HE'S ALWAYS AHEAD OF THE CROWD

When Philippe Starck, the world-famous French designer, was asked by the New York Times, why he often had such fantastic *avant-garde* ideas, he said, "I never read any magazines or watch TV nor do I go to cocktail parties, dinners or anything like that." Maybe he was *exaggerating* a bit, but anybody who knows him knows that he is certainly unconventional. He went on to say "I live alone mostly, in the middle of nowhere."

2 ____________

Philippe Starck is not the only person who wants to live *unplugged*. There is a growing number of people who are prepared to pay enormous amounts of money to stay in hotels without TVs or Internet connections. Could this be the future of tourism? These places are known as "black-hole resorts" and they are becoming more and more popular *precisely* because the guests can't go online at all.

3 WE HAVE MORE AND MORE WAYS TO COMMUNICATE, BUT LESS AND LESS TO SAY

It seems that many of us want a rest from being *constantly* connected. Surveys show that average Americans spend eight and a half hours in front of a screen every day. Many young people send or receive at least seventy text messages a day. The US may need summer camps to *rescue* children from the Internet and mobile phones soon (they already exist in South Korea and China). At the moment, children are probably sent to the camps by their parents but soon they may insist on going themselves, when they realise that videos and computer games don't *provide* them with the meaning of life.

4 ______________________

Have you ever noticed the positive effect the countryside has on you? People who go to *rural* areas on holiday away from the *hustle and bustle* of busy life are calmer and happier when they return. And they can even think better! Their attention span ist greater, their memory improves and they can solve problems more quickly and effectively. Peace and quiet is apparently necessary to be able to develop meaningful new ideas.

5 ______________________

There are of course other ways in which this can be achieved without spending *loads* of money. Try yoga or tai chi or just turn off your mobile phone every other day or at the weekend. Don't read any emails for four hours and take time every day to focus and decide what to do next. Take a walk through woods or fields or go for a bike ride without an iPod and listen to the sounds of nature. These "zoneouts" (time without any electronic connections) can help you to keep your *sanity*.

6 BE *SELFISH!* BE DISCONNECTED!

We can't all live like *monks* or *nuns* without any connections to other people. Mobile phones and computers are vital for all of us today and no-one would want to reverse progress. But we need some unconnected time to keep our balance. So take your time!

c Look at the text again and underline the words in italics. Sort them into three categories. Use your notebook and make a table like the one below.

☺ Words I know	😐 Words I'm not sure about	☹ Words I don't know

d Take your list of words, walk around, and help each other with the words you don't know.

e Read the text again and tick the correct option. Compare in small groups.

1. Philippe Starck often has new ideas because …
   - ☐ a. he gets his inspirations from astronomy.
   - ☐ b. he's disconnected from other ideas.
   - ☐ c. he meets a lot of people.

2. The average American …
   - ☐ a. watches TV and works and plays on computers for eight and a half hours a day minimum.
   - ☐ b. goes to the cinema eight times a month.
   - ☐ c. watches TV eight hours a day.

3. When you spend time in peaceful countryside areas your brain skills …
   - ☐ a. slow down.
   - ☐ b. disappear.
   - ☐ c. improve.

4. People sometimes turn off their mobile phones because …
   - ☐ a. they hate their mobile phones.
   - ☐ b. they want to be disconnected.
   - ☐ c. they want to concentrate on yoga.

5. The article says you should be selfish and …
   - ☐ a. be disconnected now and then to get your peace and quiet.
   - ☐ b. buy as many mobile phones as you like.
   - ☐ c. call everybody whenever you want.

f Would you like to spend a holiday in a black hole resort? Discuss this in small groups. What are the pros and cons?

2

a How did they keep in touch? People have always had ways of staying connected. Which forms of communication can you identify? Match the words to the pictures. Then compare with a partner.

1. ☐ telephone
2. ☐ written messages
3. ☐ airmail
4. ☐ carrier pigeon
5. ☐ email
6. ☐ smoke signals

b When was the first email sent? Look at the sentences and fill in the correct verbs. You can use each word more than once. Compare with a partner.

sent | written | made | used

1. When was the first carrier pigeon ___________ to carry messages?
2. Where was the first airmail letter ___________ from, and when?
3. Where were the first smoke signals ___________ into the air?
4. When were the first written messages ___________?
5. When was the first phone call ___________?
6. When was the first email ___________?

REMEMBER

When **was** the first phone call **made**?
The first phone call **was made** in ... (year) by ... (person).

➡ Language overview, 1.9

c Work in small groups and guess the answers in 2b.

USEFUL EXPRESSIONS

I guess this was in ...

It **might** have been ... ➡ ???
It **could** have been ... ➡ ??
It **must** have been ... ➡ ?

d Match the answers to the questions in 2b. Which answer surprised you most? Do you know any other ways of keeping in touch and passing messages on?

☐ a. In 1876, by Alexander Graham Bell und Thomas A. Watson.
☐ b. In ancient China, ancient Greece, and in North America.
☐ c. Around 5600 BC in Ancient Egypt.
☐ d. Around 4000 BC (before Christ).
☐ e. From Nassau to Miami, in 1929.
☐ f. In 1971 by Ray Tomlinson.

e Make your own quiz. Work in pairs or small groups. Write five statements, some true, some false.

The first phone call was made by Ray Tomlinson. (false)
The Lord of the Rings films were made in New Zealand. (true)

f Read out your statements. The others say if they think they are true or false. Which team has the most correct answers?

3

a Anna is sixteen years old, and her best friend is her mobile phone. This is what she uses it for.

6.30 a.m. alarm-clock
6.45 a.m. to check Facebook
7.00 a.m. to listen to favourite music in the bath
7.10 a.m. to send text messages to friends

b What do you need your mobile for? Make a list. Compare with a partner. Then compare with another pair in a group of four. What are mobiles most used for in your group?

18

c Anna's Dad is very busy in his job as an IT manager. He wants to take time out and go to a black hole resort with the family. Listen to their discussion and fill in the gaps.

1. But you can't ________________ leave my mobile phone at home!

2. Would you ________________ try diving?

REMEMBER

My parents **made me** do my homework every day.
My grandpa **let me** use his boat in the holidays.

➜ Language overview, 1.17

d Imagine you and your family / friends are planning to stay at *Maya Seaside Peace and Quiet* in Yucatan, Mexico. You would like some information before you go. You decide to call the hotel. Form two groups, A and B.

Students A: Work in a team and make a list of questions. What would you like to know before you go?

USEFUL EXPRESSIONS

Hello, this is ... speaking.
I need some information on ...
Can you tell me ...?
Is / are there any ...?
Where is ...?
How much is ...?
What kind of activities ...?
Thanks for the information.

Students B: You work at the *Maya Seaside Peace and Quiet*. Some guests are going to call you and want information. Prepare for their questions.

e Now get together in pairs, student A and student B. Make a phone call.

f What were the most interesting questions and answers?

UNIT 9

Unusual hobbies

1

a **You want to interview someone about his or her hobby. What kind of questions would you ask? Think of some questions with a partner.**

- What's your hobby?
- Why did you choose it?
- How long have you had this hobby?

REMEMBER

Why **did** you …?
How long **have** you …?
→ Language overview, 1.3, 1.4

b **Now decide which three questions are the most important for the two of you. Take a piece of paper each and write down your answers, but don't write your name on the paper.**

1. Skiing.
2. I chose it because I like the mountains.
3. For more than twenty years.

c **Your teacher collects the papers and gives you a different one. Work with a partner and guess the questions.**

- I think the second question might be "Why did you …"
- Right. And the third question probably is "How long …?"

d **Take a paper each, walk around and find the person who wrote the questions. Who has the funniest or most interesting hobby?**

2

20 a **Listen to Betty and Dorothy discussing a new hobby. What is it?**

knitting

21 b **Have you heard of this hobby? What could it be? Listen to the rest of the conversation. Number the following words in the order you hear them.**

- ☐ derelict
- ☐ mayor
- ☐ bridge railing
- ☐ cosy

c Fill in the gaps with the words from 2b.

1. A ______________ is something which is put onto a teapot or a boiled egg to keep it warm until it is time to drink the tea or eat the egg.
2. The ______________ is the person in charge of politicians who look after a town and manage its affairs.
3. ______________ is a word used for old, run-down buildings which need renovating.
4. A ______________ is necessary to stop people falling from the bridge into a river.

21

d Listen again and guess.

Guerrilla knitting is …

- ☐ a movement which started in 2004 in The Netherlands.
- ☐ meant to make our world more beautiful.
- ☐ a another term for *graffiti knitting*.
- ☐ found all over the world now.

e Betty recommends that Dorothy have her ears checked. What other advice does she give her friend?

1. You should ________ ________ ________ ________ again, dear. (do / hair)
2. Why don't you phone the cleaning lady and ________ ________ ________ ________? (clean / windows)
3. I think you need to ________ ________ ________ ________, Dorothy. You have had toothache for such a long time now! (extract / tooth)
4. You should ________ ________ ________ ________, more often, dear. It's old now and we risk a breakdown. (service / car)

REMEMBER

I need to **have** my ears **checked**.

➡ Language overview, 1.14

f Have you ever seen guerrilla knitting in your town or anywhere else? Would you join the movement? What would you knit? Discuss the questions in small groups.

3

a What hobbies do you know? In small groups, write down the alphabet on a piece of paper. Add some hobbies to the letters. Then pass the paper on to the group on your left. Check and add your own ideas. Then hang the papers on the wall. Which hobby is the most popular? Which one is the most unusual?

p a inting
b
c
rea d ing
e
f
…

b Read about Marion. Which of these statements are true?

- ☐ Marion believes that everyone should collect something.
- ☐ She collects salt and pepper containers.
- ☐ She stopped collecting after a few years as she thought she had enough.
- ☐ She doesn't keep her collection in one place.

AN INTERESTING COLLECTION

My name used to be Marion Brown but when I got married I changed my name because my husband's name was more interesting than mine – Fox. He was so pleased that I took his name that he bought me a lovely silver brooch like a fox and that started my idea for a collection. My mother-in-law actually told me that she believed everyone should collect something so she was pleased too.

She collected salt and pepper containers and had a whole cupboard full of them. She gave me two sets when I got married to her son and guess what – one set was shaped like two foxes!

I have quite a big collection of "fox-things" but I stopped collecting after a few years as I thought I had enough! There is of course the brooch and the salt and pepper set but I also have several pictures of foxes, two toy foxes, bookends, table mats, a milk jug and even a pen with a fox on the end of it. I don't keep all my collection in one place as I think that would look a bit strange. We use a lot of the things in our everyday life and I have some things in a cupboard. Of course I often wear the brooch!

c Do you know anybody who collects things? Why? What? Talk to your partner about collecting things and report back to the class. Who collects the funniest things?

MY LANGUAGE BOX

I have never tried ..., but as soon as I have enough time / money I will try it!
... has always been my biggest interest.
I have always been fascinated by ...
When I was a child I collected ...
I really enjoy ...ing.
I just love ...

d Divide the class into three groups, A, B and C. Each group reads one of the stories about unusual hobbies. In your group, help each other with words you don't know. Individually, decide on seven key words or phrases for your text and write them down.

GROUNDHOPPING

Groundhopping is a hobby that involves attending football matches at as many different stadiums as possible. The idea originated in the 1970s in England, where the magazine *Football League Review* suggested producing a special tie for supporters who visited all the ninety-two stadiums of the professional leagues. The *92 Club* was established four years later, on 2 September 1978. There are strict regulations: you need to document each stadium with date, event, team, and number of spectators. The most important rule is that you must attend a football match and not just see the stadium.

Groundhopping has now developed into a fascinating hobby which includes travelling to distant countries and meeting people who share the same hobby all over the world.

GEOCACHING

Geocaching is an outdoor activity in which the participants use a Global Positioning System (GPS) receiver to hide and seek containers, called *geo-caches* or *caches*, anywhere in the world.

A typical cache is a small waterproof container containing a logbook where the geocacher enters the date they found it and signs it with their established code name. Geocaching shares many aspects with orienteering, treasure-hunting and puzzle-solving.

Geocaches are currently placed in over 200 countries around the world and on all seven continents. After nearly thirteen years of activity there are over 1.9 million active geocaches published on various websites. There are over five million geocachers worldwide.

GEOCACHING.COM

COSPLAY

Cosplay, short for *costume play*, is a type of performance art in which participants wear costumes and accessories to represent a specific character or idea. Cosplayers often interact to create a subculture centered on role play. A broader use of the term cosplay applies to any costumed role play in venues apart from the stage, regardless of the cultural context. Favourite sources include manga and anime, comic books, video games and films.

The Internet has enabled many cosplayers to create social networks and websites centred around cosplay activities, while forums allow them to share stories, photographs, news and tips. The massive growth in the number of people picking up cosplay as a hobby since 1990 has made the phenomenon important in popular culture.

In Germany, the *Leipziger Buchmesse* is famous for the *European Cosplay Gathering* and a special Cosplay competition.

e **Close your books. Use your keywords to practise a short speech to explain the hobby.**

f **Now form new groups. Each group must have one person or more from group A, group B, and group C. Tell your group about your text and use the keywords and phrases you have written down.**

g **What do you think about these hobbies? Do you know someone who has one of these hobbies?**

h **Is there something you've always meant to do, wanted to do, but just … haven't? Matt Cutts*, a very creative software engineer at Google suggests: *Try it for thirty days*. If you had thirty days, what would you try out?**

- If I wanted to try something new for thirty days I would try *geocaching*. It must be great to be outdoors and look for hidden "treasures".
- I have always wanted to feel like Superwoman, so I would try cosplay!

* For more information on the idea of thirty day challenges go to Matt Cutts on www.TED.com.

REMEMBER

If I **wanted** to … I **would** …
If I **had** more time / money I **would** …
If my job **wasn't** so time-consuming I **would** …

➡ Language overview, 1.10

EXTRA PRACTICE

UNIT 7

1 **Do you know these words?**

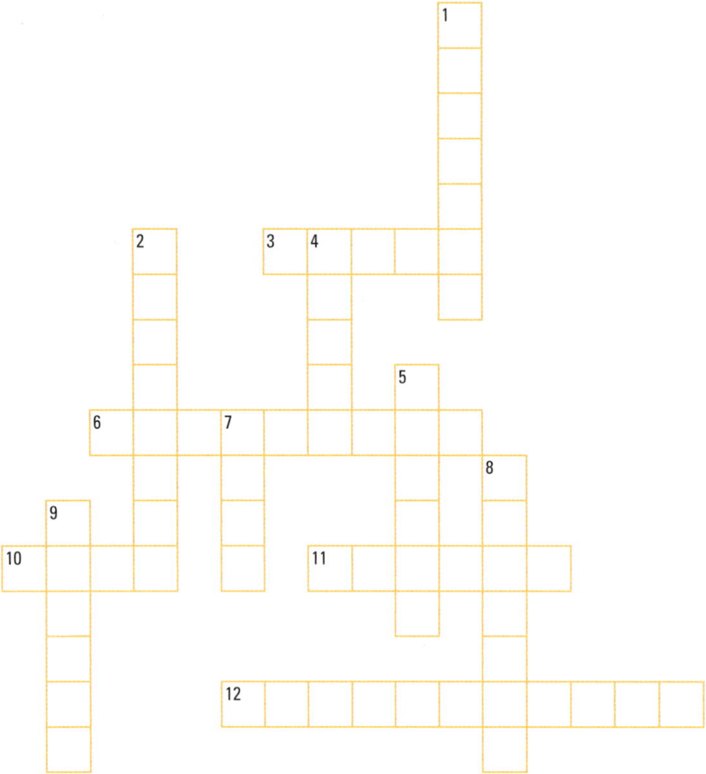

Across

3. large group of related families who live in the same area and share a common language
6. person whose profession is catching fish
10. substances such as oil or gas that produce power when burned
11. land surrounded by water
12. you need this to run cookers, radios, TVs, etc.

Down

1. used for freezing food
2. you go there when you are seriously ill
4. a large area of water that flows towards the sea
5. what you do to move a canoe
7. kill animals for food or for sport
8. advantage, profit
9. thick tropical forest

16 **2a** **Listen to Laura (Page 54) in the first part of the interview again. Number the phrases you hear in the correct order.**

- ☐ more than one million people
- ☐ supply of electrical power
- ☐ far away from civilization
- ☐ benefits of energy
- ☐ massive change

17 **2b** **Now listen to Laura in the second part of the interview. Number the phrases you hear in the correct order.**

- ☐ they produce energy without any trouble
- ☐ just in case of a power shortage
- ☐ a generator powered by fuel
- ☐ access to electrical power
- ☐ they paddle their canoes

3 **Laura is meeting Dave, her business partner from the UK. Dave is also an expert in solar energy. He travels a lot and is responsible for projects in one country. Read the following sentences. Can you guess the country?**

1. They have two famous animals which carry their babies in a pouch.
2. They have extremely long lorries there, called road trains.
3. There is a huge desert which they call the outback.
4. A traditional instrument is called the didgeridoo.
5. The British discovered this country in 1770.
6. The native people are called Aborigines.
7. They celebrate Christmas in summer.
8. The capital city is Canberra.

4 Laura is going to join Dave for a project in Melbourne but has never been to Australia before. She has a lot of questions. Fill in the correct verb forms.

1. How often *have* you *been* (be) to Australia? When ____________ (be) you there last?
2. ____________ you ever ____________ (see) kangaroos? How fast ____________ (can) they run?
3. They say koalas make noises like bulls. ____________ you ever ____________ (hear) them?
4. ____________ you ever ____________ (travel) through the outback? What ____________ you ____________ (take) for the trip?
5. I know you like operas. ____________ you ever ____________ (be) to the Sydney Opera House?
6. ____________ you ever ____________ (try) playing the didgeridoo? Can I learn to play it?

5 Dave sends an email to answer Laura's questions. Choose the correct option.

Hi Laura,

That's a lot of questions! I guess you can (1) *hard / hardly* wait to go down under! I have been (2) *to / in* Australia several times, and the last time (3) *has been / was* last Easter, which is autumn down there. I have seen a lot of kangaroos, and they can run as fast (4) *than / as* 50 kph! And they jump a distance of up to 10 m. And it's true, I have often listened to the noises of the koalas at night – you (5) *would / want* never believe that such cuddly animals can make such a noise! I have never travelled through the outback, though – it is (6) *dangerous / dangerously*, it's easy to (7) *lose / loose* your way, and you need about five litres of water per person a day to have a chance of surviving the heat. Maybe we can ask Banjora to take us on a trip (8) *some / any* time – he's a friend of mine and does guided tours of the outback, so we should be (9) *safe / safely* with him ☺. And he can play the didgeridoo as well. The didge, a beer, a campfire – sounds good, doesn't it? Opera? Why not! I have never been to the opera. Not yet! But we could go if you (10) *want to / will*!

See you soon.

Dave

6a Complete these questions about travelling. Add one more question to find out more information.

1. *Have you ever lost* (lose) your passport? *Where was it?*
2. ____________ (lose) your way in a foreign country? ____________
3. ____________ (spend) a holiday on a boat? ____________
4. ____________ (spend) the night at an airport? ____________
5. ____________ (travel) in a hot air balloon? ____________
6. ____________ (be) to a horrible hotel? ____________

6b Take your questions to class and interview some other students. Who can tell the most interesting story?

EXTRA PRACTICE UNIT 8

1 Read the definitions and find the words.

~~age~~	air	bile	ful	ga	geon	ish	maga	mail	~~mess~~	mo	peace	pi	ral	re
ru	self	sort	yo	zine										

1. message: A piece of information that you send to someone. A note, for example.
2. ______________: Physical and spiritual exercises, originally from India.
3. ______________: A small phone that you can carry around with you.
4. ______________: A journal published once a month or once a week.
5. ______________: A place that many people go to for a holiday.
6. ______________: A brown or grey bird that often lives in cities.
7. ______________: Gentle and friendly, not aggressive.
8. ______________: In the countryside, not urban.
9. ______________: A rapid mail delivery system.
10. ______________: Egoistic.

19

2a Listen to Anna and her family (Page 59) again. Anna mentions her friend, Sandra. What exactly does she say?

"I must ______________ Sandra."

2b What's the meaning of *to text* here? Read and tick.

1. ☐ Anna is planning to send a written message to Sandra using her mobile phone.
2. ☐ Anna is planning to write a long letter to her friend Sandra.

3 Anna and her friend Sandra are having a conversation. Choose the best option. Remember the examples from the recording.

1. I would never *make* / <u>*let*</u> my kids watch TV for more than sixty minutes.
2. My dad won't *let* / *make* me drive his car – he's afraid I might crash it.
3. My brother never *lets* / *makes* me use his computer. He's so selfish!
4. I hate November. It's so dark, it *makes* / *lets* me feel depressed.
5. But you can't *let* / *make* me leave my mobile phone at home!
6. My mother didn't *let* / *make* me go to the party last weekend.
7. I love going to the zoo. The monkeys *make* / *let* me laugh.
8. The police *let* / *made* my dad show his driving licence.
9. My teacher *made* / *let* me do some extra homework!
10. Would you *make* / *let* me try diving?

4a After the holiday in Mexico Anna sends an email to her friend. Do you think she liked the trip? Have a guess.

1. ☐ Yes, I think she liked it. 2. ☐ No, I don't think she liked it.

4b Read Anna's email and fill in the correct form.

Dear Sandra,

I'm back in the real world! I can phone and send emails again! I'm so happy.

But even without my mobile the holiday was really great. Imagine, we (1) were picked up (pick up) and (2) ________ (take) to the hotel in a stretch limo*! Then we (3) ________ ________ (give) a welcome cocktail – caipirinhas for my parents, and mine (4) ________ ________ (call) "Tropical Magic"! It (5) ________ ________ (make) of pears, grapefruit and banana juice with crushed ice and tonic water – yummy! Then we (6) ________ ________ (show) our room – Dad had booked a suite for us! We went to the beach, and I …

*stretch limo = an extra long, very comfortable limousine car

5 Sandra wants to go to Mexico too. She wants to learn Spanish at a language school there. Look at the website and put the phone call in the correct order.

Phone SPANISH CENTRE now:
0-800-404 770986

Mexico is the most populous Spanish-speaking country in the world, with a population of about 112 million inhabitants. The people are friendly and warm-hearted. We have impressive colonial towns, wonderful wildlife, and a fantastic countryside between the Pacific Ocean, the Gulf of Mexico and the Caribbean Sea!

Learn Spanish in Mexico and experience this magnificent and enchanting country!

- ☐ So that would be a beginner's course. I can send you an offer for a three-week course with flight and accommodation with a host family here in Playa del Carmen. Can you give me your email address? I'll send you the information then.
- ☐ Hello, this is Sandra speaking from Germany. I need some information on language learning courses.
- ☐ Of course! My address is sandrahei@yahoo.com. Thanks for the information!
- ☐ In our summer holidays, August or September.
- ☐ How long would you like to stay?
- ☐ Well, it depends on the price. I can't spend more than €1,800, and I would like to have lessons in the morning and excursions in the afternoon.
- ☐ I can understand a bit because I had Latin at school, but I can't speak it.
- 1 Spanish Centre Playa del Carmen, Luisa speaking. How can I help you?
- ☐ OK, let me see … What level are you?
- ☐ Wonderful! When would you like to come to Mexico?
- ☐ Your're welcome! Hasta luego.

EXTRA PRACTICE UNIT 9

1 **Betty and Dorothy (Page 60) enjoy doing word games. Join them and make a word snake. Use the last letter of a word as the first letter of the next one.**

SKIING – GARDEN – NOVEMBER – RUN-DOWN – NEED – D …

Now try and make a really long word snake. The word list on page 134 might help you. Who can make the longest word snake?

2 **It'll be Dorothy's birthday soon. Betty would like to give her a present but doesn't have any ideas. She tries to find out what her friend might need. Write questions using the following items.**

~~old-fashioned pair of glasses~~	worn-out pullover	old handbag	awful watch	old coat

How long have you had this old-fashioned pair of glasses, dear?

How long have ____________________

____

____

____

3a (22) **In their conversation Dorothy and Betty are discussing guerrilla knitting. Listen and complete the sentences.**

1. Do you ________ ________ it's very cold at the zoo?
2. Don't ________ ________ it's a really depressing view?
3. I'm ________ ________ ________ of this hopeless grey town!
4. ________ it is not quite legal …
5. On the ________ ________, it sounds rather exciting …

3b **Now use the sentence beginnings and finish them with your own ideas.**

1. Do you really think *cosplay is interesting? I guess it's awfully boring!*
2. Don't you agree ____________________
3. I'm sick and tired of ____________________
4. Actually ____________________
5. On the other hand, ____________________

4a Look at the picture, read and tick the correct option.

- ☐ Dorothy is having her hair cut.
- ☐ Dorothy is cutting her hair.

4b Dorothy and Betty are planning to meet up with the guerrilla knitting club in London. But before they leave, a lot of things need to be done. Look at their to-do list and make sentences.

Dorothy:

1. I need a new railcard. I must have *my picture taken* (picture / my / taken).
2. I would like to leave a key with the neighbour. We should __________ (a spare key / have / made).
3. My coat is dirty. I should __________ (it / cleaned / have) before we go.

Betty:

1. The washing machine is leaking. We need to __________ (it / fixed / have).
2. The car is so old – we must __________ (serviced / it / have) before we go.
3. Dorothy looks so good now with her new haircut – I need to __________ (cut / my / hair / have), too!

5 In London they decide to go to the bingo hall and try their luck. What would they do if they won £10,000? Fill in the correct form of the verb and add two more sentences.

1. If we *won* (win) £10,000 we would buy a lot of wool.
2. If we __________ (have) a lot of wool we would knit nice scarves and sell them.
3. If we __________ (have) a lot of money we would buy a new car.
4. If we __________ (have) a new car we would travel to Germany.
5. If we __________ (travel) to Germany we would visit the Oktoberfest.
6. If we __________ (visit) __________

____

6 What would you do if you had a lot of money? Write a few sentences. Are there any people in the class who have the same ideas?

FRIENDSHIP SCARVES

You've heard of friendship rings, friendship bands and now you can buy friendship scarves for anyone you care about or love. The company which makes them is owned by two friends, Patricia Hodbury and Marjorie Newsome (Pat and Marj). You can buy a scarf for the summer in cotton or for the winter in wool and there are no two scarves which are the same. The company is called Neckwear and the idea came about when Pat and Marj were telling their daughters, Alicia and Amy, about their schooldays in the 1970s in England. Each school had a uniform in those days with a scarf in the school colours as part of it. Boyfriends and girlfriends exchanged scarves, so if a girl had a boyfriend, she wore his scarf. It wasn't allowed at school of course, but after school and at the weekends it was a very popular thing to do. Pat and Marjorie both wore their boyfriends' scarves and both still have them as they are both married to their boyfriends from school days, Dick and Dave!! They don't wear the scarves anymore because they think school scarves would look silly on women of fifty-something, but they are both proud of the scarves and think they are a sign of a long love and friendship.

When they told their daughters about the scarves, Alicia said she wanted a scarf for her boyfriend, Chris. But she didn't want a school scarf! So Pat knitted her one and added a special feature. When

Amy, Marjorie's daughter saw the scarf, she immediately wanted one for her boyfriend, Enrico. And then they knitted scarves for their daughters' friends (and their boyfriends). The mothers never thought of selling the scarves until one day someone at Amy's school asked if she could buy one. Their idea was born of starting a company and knitting friendship scarves for anyone who wants one.

Customers choose how long and how wide they want the scarf to be and the colours they want. The price depends on all these things. And the special feature? Each scarf has two names (the names of the friends) knitted into the edge. If the names have letters which are the same, they are joined together. You can order the scarves for a boyfriend, girlfriend, husband or wife and each one is absolutely unique.

Pat and Marj sell their scarves through an Internet portal called *Loobiedoobie* which specialises in home-made clothes and accessories. They didn't have to invest much as each scarf is made to order. And the orders keep coming and coming …

Both Pat and Marj share all the work and the knitting and they have so many orders coming in that they are thinking about taking on new knitting partners. So if there are any passionate knitters out there, just get in touch!

TWO MUMS KNIT AND NATTER*

What better way to make money than doing something you are good at and love for people who love each other? That's what Pat and Marj, two mums from Manchester, started doing six months ago. Now everyone wants a friendship scarf for their best friend or loved one. Of course there is a discount if you buy two! Choose your colours, size and material and place your order. Each scarf has a special feature which is ...

* Informal word for talk, chat.

Describing things

It's … cm high / … cm long / … cm wide.
It's made of metal / plastic / wood.
You need it for making …
You use it to make …
It's someone who …
It's something which …
It's kind of a …

Asking for information

I need some information on …
Can you tell me …?
Is / are there any …?
Where is …?
How much is …?
What kind of …?

Talking about change

I used to take the car to go to work, but now I …
Solar energy is the solution.
More and more people turn to yoga.
Some people turn off their online connections all weekend.
Be selfish! Be disconnected!
It's vital, of course, to stay in touch with the world.
When you spend time relaxing, your brain skills improve.
Where was the first airmail letter written from and when?
When was the first carrier pigeon used to carry messages?
Guerrilla knitting is meant to make our world more beautiful.
If I had more time / money I would …
If my job wasn't so time-consuming I would …

Talking about past experiences

Have you ever been to Asia?
When was that?
I have been to America several times. The first time I went …
I have never been to Canada. But I certainly would like to go!
My parents made me practise the piano every day.
My grandmother let me bake cakes with her in the holidays.

My useful expression corner

USEFUL EXPRESSIONS

I'm not sure, but the text might tell us something about …
Sorry? I didn't really get that.
… has always been my biggest interest.
I have always been fascinated by …
I really enjoy …ing.
I just love …ing …
I really should have my hair done.
I must have my house / windows cleaned soon.

Add some other useful expressions from Module 3 that you want to remember.

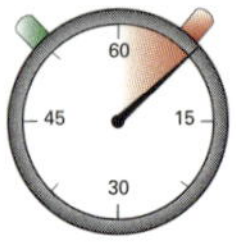

Look back at what you have done in Module 3 and prepare a one-minute talk about your hobby. Talk about what it is, when and why you started it, why you like it and any other details.

Track your progress

Read the following checklist and tick a smiley.

Now I can …	☺	😐	☹
… describe something if I don't know the word.			
… ask someone to repeat something if I don't understand.			
… say what I used to do and what I do now.			
… guess the meaning of unfamiliar words in a text.			
… talk about ways of keeping in touch.			
… say when something was done for the first time.			
… talk about dates in the past.			
… describe what I need something for.			
… say what someone makes me do and lets me do.			
… inquire about information I need (on the telephone).			
… ask someone about their hobby.			
… ask someone how long they have had something.			
… say I need to have something done.			
… recommend that someone has something done.			
… describe what I would do if I had more time or money.			

Think about the following questions and discuss them with a partner.

What was new for you? What did you remember? What would you like to do better?
What was the most difficult thing to learn?

Work 4

Jobs and languages
Work and communication
What next?

Jobs and languages

1

a What words do you associate with work? With a partner, think of words and put them in three groups. Use your notebook.

☺	😐	☹
pleasant		

USEFUL EXPRESSIONS

Work is meaningful.
necessary.
enjoyable.
pleasant.
healthy.
It's good to have a routine.
Work gives you a purpose.
Work keeps you active.

23

b Listen to these people talking about work and match the pictures to the texts.

23

c Listen again to Juliet, Charlotte, David, and Sam. Who says what? Fill in the names.

1. ________________ works only to earn money.
2. ________________ works as little as possible.
3. ________________ would like to retire now.
4. ________________ has a permanent job.
5. ________________ has a temporary job.
6. ________________ works freelance.

d Which of the four people would you change places with? Why?

MY LANGUAGE BOX

I would prefer to be employed than be freelance.
I wish I could give up my job because …
I would like to do Juliet's job because …
If I had a lot of money, I would …

e What is work for you? With a partner, tick or add what you think and explain why.

Work is something I …

- ☐ only do to earn money.
- ☐ enjoy doing.
- ☐ would like to do more.
- ☐ hate.

____

REMEMBER

What do you do? = What is your job?

➜ Language overview, 1.1

2

a Who does what as a part of their job? Match job and activity.

1. make phone calls ☐

g. a waiter

2. eat and drink ☐

h. a call centre operator

b. a pilot

3. take photos ☐

4. advise ☐

f. a restaurant critic

e. a chambermaid

5. serve ☐

c. a journalist

a. a personal shopper

6. clean ☐

7. write ☐

8. fly ☐

d. a photographer

b Read the definitions and add the jobs.

1. A ______________________ has to eat and drink as part of his / her job.
2. A ______________________ helps people to decide what to buy.
3. A ______________________ brings food and drink to customers.
4. A ______________________ often sees his / her name in print.
5. A ______________________ spends a lot of time in the air.
6. A ______________________ cleans and tidies bedrooms.
7. A ______________________ talks a lot on the telephone.
8. A ______________________ needs equipment to work.

c Choose one of the jobs above. Work with a partner. Ask each other questions about the job you have chosen.

USEFUL EXPRESSIONS

What do you do every day?
What did you learn in your training?
Do you have special qualifications?
What are you good at?
What do you hate?
What do you never do?
What would you change if you could?

d Report back to the group. Would you like to do these jobs? Why? Why not? Could you do these jobs?

USEFUL EXPRESSIONS

I wouldn't like to be a chambermaid because I hate cleaning.
I could be a personal shopper because I like talking to people.
I couldn't be a waiter because I am a bit clumsy.

e With a partner, think of an unusual job and write a short definition. Swap definitions with another pair and see if you can guess the job. Continue until you have read all the definitions. Which job is the most unusual? What questions would you ask these people about their jobs?

3

a **In which of the following countries is English an official language? What other languages are spoken there? Discuss with a partner.**

REMEMBER

English is spoken in …

Language overview, 1.1

Wales · India · Canada · South Africa · Sweden · Ghana · China

b **Now read the following website and match the country to the description.**

English around the world

1. India: A hundred different languages are spoken here, including Malayalam, Urdu and Gujerati. English is one of two official languages.
2. ______: English is one of the two official languages, but 71% understand and speak only English and not the other language. However almost everything official is printed in both languages.
3. ______: The two official languages are English and French, but 21% of the population have a mother tongue which is not English or French.
4. ______: There are eleven official languages, including English, Sesotho and isiXhosa.
5. ______: There are seventy-nine languages, including Akan, Abron, Ga and Hausa. The official language is English. Most people are bilingual and many speak three or four languages fluently.
6. ______: There is only one official language. Other languages are recognised in different regions, but English is not one of them.
7. ______: There is one official language which is not English but 80% of the people speak English as a foreign language.

c **Read the following text. Do you agree? Discuss the text with a partner.**

INTERNATIONAL ENGLISH

It seems that 80% of all business conversations in English now take place without any native speakers present. English is spoken by a lot of people who have learnt it as a second or foreign language. What does this mean for English learners? If you want other people to understand you, maybe you should forget some of the things you learnt in school. Here are some tips if you want to use International English.

- Don't worry too much about the sound *th* in English. Many native speakers

cannot pronounce it and it is usually not important for the meaning. ➔➔➔

- Correct vocabulary is more important than correct grammar.
- Be very careful with false friends as they often cause confusion.
- Don't use too many idioms, sayings or proverbs. Not everybody will understand them.
- Don't worry about making mistakes.
- Practise listening to different accents.
- Learn ways of asking for help.
- Learn polite language which everyone will understand.

24

d Listen to these three people. Who do you find easiest to understand? Who is most difficult? Can you complete the sentences?

1. Seiko thinks that she is ________________ to understand.
   She wants to improve her ________________.
2. Olga says people find her ________________ to understand.
   She wants to improve her ________________.
3. Fabian says people usually find him ________________ to understand
   but he would like to improve his ________________.

e What about your English? What would you like to improve? Discuss with a partner.

f What do you need English (or other languages) for? With a partner, tick and add your own needs.

MY LANGUAGE BOX

I need English …
I want to improve my English for …

- ☐ on the telephone
- ☐ presentations
- ☐ negotiations
- ☐ interpreting
- ☐ translation
- ☐ travelling
- ☐ emails
- ☐ letters
- ________________

4

a Can you use these words correctly? Match them to their definitions. With a partner, make sentences to show what the words mean. Can you think of any more false friends?

1. eventually
2. pension
3. actually
4. brief
5. chef
6. note
7. rent

a. money you get when you retire
b. money you pay for a flat
c. professional cook
d. short letter
e. at the end
f. in fact
g. short

■ He knows a lot about cooking. He's a chef in a very good restaurant.

b With a partner, think of English words you use in your own language in a work context. Who can get the most in two minutes?

■ What about *Marketing*, *E-Business*, …?

▼ Yes, or *Smartphone*, …

c Here are some German words which are used in other languages. Do you know any more? Work with a partner.

Waldsterben, Autobahn, Kaffeeklatsching

Work and communication

1

a **Is it work when a bird builds a nest? Is it work when a wife makes herself attractive for her husband? Discuss these questions with your partner.**

b **And what about the questions on the right? Tick what you think is work. Then compare and discuss with your partner.**

Is it work when you …
- ☐ take part in an English course in your company?
- ☐ go to the pub with colleagues after work?
- ☐ have a break for a cigarette or a coffee?
- ☐ look for a holiday on the Internet?
- ☐ write an email to a friend at work?
- ☐ go on a company outing?

c **Do these people work? Read and decide on your answer and discuss in small groups.**

aboutwork.com

Roger, 67 I'm officially a pensioner now. Well, I lost my job seven years ago when the company I directed closed down. And then I started my own company advising businesses. I also write articles about business topics. I earn money from the first job but not the second. It is just nice to see my name in print! I don't really need the money as I got quite a big golden handshake and I also get a pension but I need something to do to keep my mind and body active. My wife still goes out to work so we share the housework but that wouldn't be enough for me.

Britta, 52 I had plenty to do when my three children were small but as they got older, I had too much time on my hands and started to get a bit bored. I used to be a nurse but the work would be too physically hard for me now. So I thought about what I am good at and now I look after other children in my house. It doesn't feel like work and I even earn regular money doing something I enjoy. I also have a daily routine which I really need.

Jim, 60 I worked in a factory for thirty years but had to stop ten years ago for health reasons. I needed something to do so I started cleaning and doing work for old people and found that I enjoyed it very much. I clean, go shopping for them, sometimes cook and do small things for them in their homes. Sometimes I just talk to them or we play cards or Scrabble. It gives my life a meaning and although I don't earn a lot, I feel that I am doing something necessary.

d Read again and add more words to the table.

Money	Workplaces	Activities
golden handshake	company	advising

e Which activities do you do regularly? Which do you think are work? Which are pleasure?

REMEMBER

I started working / looking after …
I look after customers.
I used to work …
I work at home.
I had to …
I still …

➡ Language overview, 1.1, 1.6, 1.13, 1.15, 1.16

2

a Read the emails written by people at work and match them to the situations.

- ☐ replying to a job application
- ☐ spending free time together
- ☐ refusing an invitation
- ☐ asking a favour

To: Melissa
Cc:
Subject: sorry

Dear Melissa,
I am sorry I won't be able to come to the meeting as I am on holiday that week.
Best wishes,
Helen

1

To: Viola
Cc:
Subject: yoga

Hi Viola,
No, I don't think I am going to yoga today as I think I can feel a cold coming on. Is Sandra here? I haven't seen her today. Maybe see you later.
Judith

2

To: John Black
Cc:
Subject: your application as trainer

Dear Mr Black,
Thank you very much for your application as a trainer at our institution. At present we are able to cover all our needs with our existing team so do not require your services. We will contact you if a position becomes vacant.
With best wishes,
Dr. Silvia Martin

3

To: Alex
Cc:
Subject: Could you do me a favour?

Hi Alex,
Could you possibly stand in for me next Monday? I would be really grateful as it's my Mum's 60th birthday and I'd love to go her party. I'm sure she'd like to hear a speech from her favourite son! Of course, I'll return the favour and take over your shift sometime. Just ask me!
All the best,
Gabriel

4

b Look at the different ways of beginning and ending the emails. Decide what is formal and what is informal.

formal	
informal	Hi

UNIT 11

c In pairs, write an email in reply to email 4.

d What emails do you write regularly in English?

USEFUL EXPRESSIONS

Dear …	Best wishes
Hi …	With best wishes
	All the best
I'm afraid I can't …	I'd love to …
Of course I will …	

3

(27)

a Would you like to travel for your work? How do these people feel about travel and work? Listen and write down what Ralph, Marianne, Dieter and Vicki say. Use your notebook.

Ralph	
Marianne	
Dieter	
Vicki	

b Now work in groups. Half the class thinks of the positive things about travelling for work and half the class thinks of the negative things. Which group has the most arguments?

MY LANGUAGE BOX

I think that travelling for work is exciting.
Well, I find travelling stressful.
I sometimes get fed up with travelling.
I would hate to travel for work.
I would love to travel more.

c With a partner, think of all the things that can go wrong when you are travelling.

USEFUL EXPRESSIONS

The satnav doesn't work properly.
The hotel is dirty / cold / noisy.
There is no Internet access.
You lose your ticket.
Your flight is cancelled.
You might become ill.

d Your boss recently made a business trip to Scotland with Britair. His return flight was cancelled and he had to stay an extra night in a hotel and missed an important meeting. He has asked you to write to the airline and complain. With a partner, write an email to the airline. Use the details below. Begin and end the email in an appropriate way.

Cancelled flight No. BR546 Aberdeen – Stuttgart on January 15th 20..., 16:00
Hotel costs: £120, Royal Scotland Hotel, Aberdeen

USEFUL EXPRESSIONS

I am writing to …
I would like you to

4

a **Read the following definition of *negotiation*. With a partner, think of when you last negotiated something.**

A **negotiation** takes place when two or more people have different ideas, aims and needs and want to or have to agree. They try to find an agreement in a discussion. A negotiation can be between a parent and a child about when to come home at night, between a boss and an employee about a salary or a pay rise, or a customer and a company about the price of something.

28

b **Listen to the following negotiations and complete the sentences.**

1. Chris wants to stay out until *midnight* ____________________

   Pamela thinks he should come home at ____________________

   They agree on ____________________

2. The customer is unhappy about ____________________

   The shop assistant offers ____________________

   They agree on ____________________

3. The customer asks for ____________________

   The mobile phone provider says they can ____________________

   They agree on ____________________

4. He wants ____________________

   She would prefer ____________________

   They agree on ____________________

28

c **Listen again and match the beginnings and the endings of the expressions.**

1. I can offer you a	a. go down a bit with the price.
2. I would really	b. offer me a similar price?
3. That is really	c. prefer a discount.
4. That sounds	d. discount of 5%.
5. I think I can	e. think about it.
6. I'll have to	f. agree to that.
7. Can you	g. much better.
8. We can	h. too late.

d **Choose one of the situations from b for the whole class. Work in two groups. Each group prepares one part. Then find a partner from the other group and act out the negotiation.**

USEFUL EXPRESSIONS

You can stay until midnight if I pick you up.
I would like to suggest …
How much would you like to pay?
If you …, then I will …
Can you give me a lower price?
I can do that if you …
I'm afraid that is not possible.

UNIT 12

What next?

1

a Match the photos and the words.

1. sack gardens

4. home office

3. Twitter

2. email scams

b Will these things be more or less important in the future?

- Sack gardens will be more important because there is less and less space in the cities.

REMEMBER

more important **than**
most important
as important **as**

less important **than**
least important

➜ Language overview, 2.1

c Can you answer the questions? Discuss them in pairs.

1. What equipment or devices do you need to use Twitter?
2. Where do the words *twitter* and *tweeting* come from?
3. What do criminals use email scams for?
4. What are sack gardens used for?
5. Why do many people like to work from home nowadays?

d Read this information and check whether your answers in 1b and 1c were right.

Twitter is used for passing on short pieces of news quickly to lots of followers. You only need a mobile phone but you can tweet from a PC too. Messages can not be more than 140 characters. The words *twitter* and *tweet* come from the sounds birds make.

Email scams are to make money for criminals but no-one really knows how successful they are. People think they can get something for nothing and believe in get-rich-quick schemes and "too good to be true" investments. Many people have lost their life savings because of email scams.

Home offices – Many people would like to stop travelling to work so they choose, if they can, to telecommute and work from home. Over five million people in the US work at home regularly and more from time to time. Some are self-employed but many employees use this alternative work arrangement.

A **sack garden** is very simple to make at home if you don't have much garden space. You can plant flowers, vegetables or fruit in one. They are useful in developing countries and poor urban areas. The sacks can be made of plastic or cloth.

e **Get together with another pair. Compare your answers and talk about your experience with these things. Discuss the following questions.**

1. Have you ever used Twitter?
2. What can you do about email scams?
3. Have you ever seen a sack garden?
4. What are the pros and cons of home offices?

USEFUL EXPRESSIONS

I (would) never use Twitter.
I know something about home offices.
I have never seen an email like this.
I think this is a great idea.
I would like to try this.
I have never experienced anything like this.
This happened to me only yesterday.

2

30

a **Listen to Naomi talking about her technology history and future and complete the life line.**

cassette player · first mobile · first TV · first notebook · smartphone · iPad

when I was five	______
when I was fifteen	______
when I was sixteen	______
when I was eighteen	______
two years ago	______
today	
future	______

MY LANGUAGE BOX

I got my first …
I have never had a …
I'm getting a … next month.
I started …

b **What topic is this life line on the right about?**

☐ job ☐ family ☐ money

met my first wife
got engaged
married
divorced
met second partner
moved together
married
1st child born
2nd child born
bought own house
today

c **Choose one of these topics (or any other one) and make your own life line. Now interview your partner and find out about his / her history. Explain your life line.**

technology · environment · money · work · family

REMEMBER

When did you …?
Why did you decide to …?

➡ Language overview, 1.3

d **What is the most interesting piece of information you heard?**

- I think the most interesting information is that …

3

31 **a** **Listen to these people talking about the future. What topics are they talking about? Use your notebook and fill in the table.**

	positive	negative
Food		

31 **b** **Listen again. What do they think will be positive and negative?**

c **How have these things changed for you in the last twenty years? How will they change?**

MY LANGUAGE BOX

I used to get money from the bank cashier but now I get it from a cash machine.
Soon we won't need money at all.
When I was in school we didn't use computers at all.
I don't need to carry a dictionary with me now.

housework and cooking · driving · banking · smart phone · learning · iPad

d **Read this text about how the use of English has changed. Then match the columns *German word* and *Correct English translation*.**

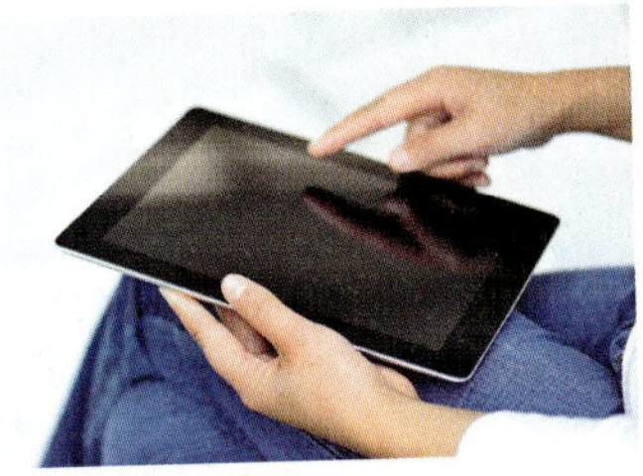

Be careful – not everything which looks English is English!

Forty years ago, there were only a few English words used in German. A well-known example is *old-timer* which meant a completely different thing from the original English word. Nowadays it is almost impossible to read anything without English words – or words which look and sound English like *beamer* and *handy*. But if you use these false friends in English, you will not always be understood correctly. There are also German words which are similar to English words but mean something different like *become*, *eventually* and *actually*.
The good news is that there are also best friends like *authentic*, *illegal* and *organization* which look and mean the same in both languages. And there are new friends – new English words like *tablet* meaning the same in English and German. Does this all make learning English easier?

German word
1. bekommen
2. eventuell
3. Oldtimer
4. Beamer
5. aktuell
6. Handy

Correct English translation
a. mobile phone
b. projector
c. possible
d. current
e. vintage car
f. to get

Senior citizen with vintage car

e **How many friends (false, best or new) can you think of? Look through the book to find as many as you can.**

4

a How has your English changed since you started this course? What can you do now?

Can you give a nice reply if you are caught speeding by the police in Australia?
Can you help your son / daughter / grandchild with his / her homework?
Can you write a plan for your retirement in New Zealand?
Can you go to California as an au pair grandma?
Can you write an email to someone in China?

b Can your partner do the same things as you? What can most people in the class do?

c With a partner or in a group, choose one of the following situations. Decide who is speaking and what they say. Make up a conversation. You can write it down if you want. Then act it for the others. Which is the funniest / best?

Telephone an organic food company and ask for information.
Give advice on the best way to spend or invest € 5,000.
Design a survey about feeling happy.
Book a holiday in an unusual holiday resort.

5

a Imagine you want to have a reunion of your English class. In groups, plan the reunion.

When do you want to meet?
Where will you meet?
What can you do?
What can you eat / drink?
Should everyone bring something?
What language will you speak?

b Now write an invitation to the reunion. Remember all the important details.

c What are you going to do next (tomorrow, after this course, next month, next year)?

MY LANGUAGE BOX

I'm (definitely) going to …
I think I will …
I'm not sure …
I might …

EXTRA PRACTICE UNIT 10

1 What's the odd one out?

1. qualification / customer / training / certificate / grammar school
2. barman / pilot / chambermaid / waiter / chef
3. language / idiom / pension / native speaker / proverb
4. enjoyable / job / pleasant / temporary / permanent
5. Sweden / Welsh / China / South Africa / Canada

25

2 Charlotte (Page 74) used to work in marketing but has changed her life a lot. Listen again and tick if the sentences are true or false.

	true	false
1. Charlotte left university three years ago.	☐	☐
2. She travels with her partner.	☐	☐
3. They decided travelling is their top priority.	☐	☐
4. They work as teachers, maid and waiter.	☐	☐
5. Their next destination is Africa.	☐	☐

26

3a Juliet, David and Sam (Page 74) decided on a different lifestyle. Listen again and fill in the gaps.

live on the rent | freelance | colleagues | standard of living | ~~retire~~
meaningful | earn | freedom | enough work | home office | inherited

Juliet: Hi, I'm Juliet. I have a wonderful job which I enjoy, but if I could (1) retire tomorrow, I would. I do interesting work, (2) __________ a good salary, have a great boss and very pleasant (3) __________ and have flexible working hours and a (4) __________ __________ so can work more or less when I want. Of course I …

David: I'm David. I work as a (5) __________ translator and only work when I need to. I live alone in a small flat and don't have a high (6) __________ __________ __________ so I often refuse work if I don't need the money. I enjoy the (7) __________ my work gives me and so I usually only …

Sam: Hi, my name's Sam. I (8) __________ some houses from my grandfather and can (9) ________ ________ ________ ________ which I get from them so I don't need to work. Of course, it is nice having enough money to live on without working but I have to find (10) __________ things to do with my time. I can draw very well so I draw pictures for children's books which is fun and I can do it whenever I want. My wife and I go on holiday a lot and I like working in the house and garden, not cleaning and so on, but designing and decorating. That's (11) __________ __________ for me.

3b Find the sentences.

1. *Juliet:* I have a wonderful job which I enjoy, but if I could retire tomorrow, I would.
   could / wish / I / soon / retire / I

   I wish ______________________________

2. *Juliet:* Of course I need the money but there are so many other things I would like to do with my time.
   time / I / If / had / things / more / I / like / would / to / many / other / do

   If I had more ______________________________

3. *David:* I enjoy the freedom my work gives me and so I usually only work about twenty-five hours a week.
   money / If / I / more / I / not / would / happier / had / be

   If I ______________________________

4. *David:* I enjoy the other things in life too much.
   I / change / wouldn't / my / want / life / to

   I ______________________________

5. *Sam:* I inherited some houses from my grandfather and can live on the rent which I get from them so I don't need to work.
   houses / I / didn't / If / any / I / would / have / have / work / to

   If I didn't ______________________________

6. *Sam:* I can draw very well so I draw pictures for children's books which is fun.
   draw / If / I / didn't / pictures / for / my / children's books / life / be / less meaningful / would

   If I didn't draw ______________________________

4 Now make a quiz for your classmates! Write six statements (as in 2) about Juliet, David, and Sam. Some of them should be true, some false. Bring them to class. The other students have to say which sentences are true and which are false.

5 And one more quiz! Here are some words which have "travelled" from German into other languages. Match them to the German original and the English meaning.

1. Vahtimestari (Finnish)	a. U-Boot	German Oktoberfest music
2. Arbeito (Japanese)	b. Wachtmeister	small window in the door, used to check who the visitor is
3. Besservisseri (Finnish)	c. Was ist das	additional job
4. Vasistas (French)	d. Besserwisser	a boat you cannot see because it moves under water
5. Kanitzeen Boot (Afrikaans)	e. bayrische Blasmusik	security guard
6. Oom pah pah (Australian English)	f. Arbeit	know-it-all

EXTRA PRACTICE UNIT 11

1a Useful phrases connected with work – connect the two halves of the sentences.

1. Do you sometimes write articles
2. When I was between jobs I had
3. A few years ago I had to stop
4. Do you often have a break
5. When I am at work I never
6. Could you possibly stand
7. How often do you write
8. Have you ever been
9. I have been
10. I will be

a. in an English course for three years now.
b. look for a holiday on the Internet!
c. too much time on my hands.
d. working for health reasons.
e. emails to friends at work?
f. in for me next Monday?
g. on a company outing?
h. about business topics?
i. on holiday next week.
j. for a cigarette?

1b Choose three expressions from 1a and write sentences about yourself.

I have a break for a cigarette every three hours.

____

____

____

1c Bring your sentences to class and compare them with others. Who has the most sentences which are similar to yours?

2a Do you know the words?

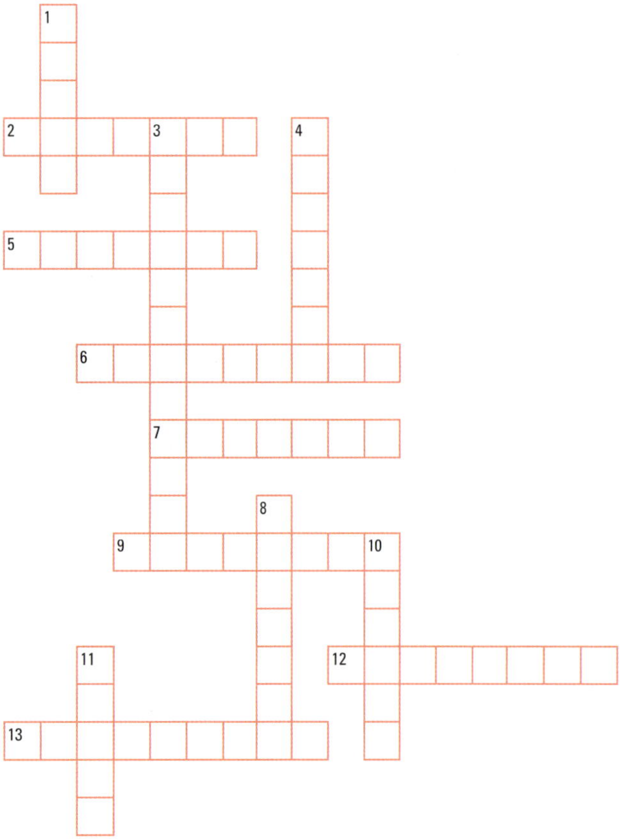

Across
2. time off, vacation
5. another word for firm
6. driver
7. traveller, visitor
9. conferences
12. another word for gifts
13. traveller who rides in someone else's vehicle

Down
1. the person who flies a plane
3. the opposite of advantage
4. unusual, extraordinary
8. smaller than a town
10. frightened, afraid
11. go and see someone

2b **Listen to Ralph, Marianne, Dieter and Vicki (Page 80) again and write the words from the crossword in the gaps. One word is not in the crossword. Which one is it?**

Ralph: I'm a (1) ________ so my job is travelling. So I couldn't do it if I didn't like travelling. I love flying but only if I am in charge of the plane and definitely not as a passenger. I have been flying long haul flights for ten years now and have seen very many interesting places. It's great to visit somewhere like Delhi in India for a few days and then return as a (2) ________ with my wife. I think I have the perfect job as I can plan my holidays as part of my work. The only (3) ________ is that when I travel on (4) ________, I have to be a (5) ________ on a plane!

Marianne: I don't like flying and would hate to travel for my work. I have only flown once because we wanted to (6) ________ my daughter in America and I was really (7) ________. So travelling far away is not for me. I'm a real home lover and my work as a checkout assistant at a supermarket in my (8) ________ suits me fine. I can …

Dieter: My job is Head of Facilities and I look after the technical side of things in the (9) ________ and sometimes I drive the boss to (10) ________ in different parts of the country. I'm not really a (11) ________ but as I really enjoy driving, I think it might be a good job to have. I can …

Vicki: I never thought writing a book could mean so much (12) ________. A year ago, I wrote a best-seller about a young mother and now I travel around and read from my book. I stay in some really (13) ________ places, sometimes in hotels and sometimes in people's homes, but it all very interesting. I'm usually only away from home for a night so my family can manage without me and I can bring my children nice (14) ________. …

3a **Vicki was travelling to read from her book but had a very unpleasant experience. Read her email to her friend Cora.**

Hi Cora,
How are you? I hope life is good to you ;) I have a horrible cold, and guess why? Yes, it's National Rail – again! I was on my way to Nottingham, and of course there was a delay – technical problems, the usual thing. I had to wait for four hours! The waiting room was unheated. They have to save money, said the service person ☹. You know what? I read an article about high class hotels which rent rooms by the hour for exhausted business travellers, and I'm going to ask my publisher if they are willing to pay for it – or if they want an author with a runny nose for the rest of their lives ☺. Will do that right away! I'll keep you posted.
Take care. Love, Vicki

Dear Mr Turner,
I am writing today …

3b **Now write Vicki's email to the publisher. Remember to use formal phrases. Take your email to class and choose the best one.**

EXTRA PRACTICE UNIT 12

1a **Find ten words from the unit in the word snake.**

TWITTEREMAILENGAGEDDEVICEORGANICOLDTIMERSAVINGSEVENTUALLYENVIRONMENTTECHNOLOGY

1b **Match the halves and make complete words. More than one combination is possible.**

~~sack~~	cassette	organic	known	player	countries
home	email	self-	employed	~~garden~~	food
developing	well-	hospital	soaps	office	scam

sack garden

1c **Choose two words from 1a and 1b and write sentences about yourself.**

If I was self-employed I would have more free time.

1d **Compare your sentences with another student. Did he / she choose the same words?**

32 **2a** **Listen to Naomi (Page 83) again. Which of the words in 1a and 1b does she use?**

33 **2b** **Listen to Chris, Helen and Tony (Page 84) again and underline the correct word.**

Chris: ... Don't you think people will think more about healthy eating? So, we'll probably eat less meat and more organically grown (1) *fruit / food* and vegetables?

Helen: I don't know really, there are so many scandals happening that I don't believe a lot of what it says in adverts. I think people will go for the cheapest (2) *foot / food* and hope for the best.

Chris: Well, I definitely eat less prepared food and make more myself so I know what is in what I eat – no old meat or (3) *horsemeat / horse meet* for instance.

Helen: I think maybe no meat at all is the best way but I just love a steak now and again. I even know (4) *vegetarians / vegetables* who say that!

Tony: I know I eat much more exotic food than my parents did. We go to Korean, Thai, Indian and African restaurants and often (5) *no / know* all about the food even though we've never been to the countries.

Helen: But travel is (6) *also / although* becoming so much cheaper and easier. People travel all over the world nowadays. That's a real advantage to globalization.

Tony: Yeah, but I think sometimes tourists forget that cultures are still different and behave in ways which upset people or are even dangerous. There are still a lot of poor (7) *people / pupils* in the world even if tourism brings (8) *money / many* into their countries. Tourism has meant more crime in some countries. And I heard that Internet crime often starts in poorer countries. People can earn money, for instance, (9) *buy / by* writing these emails promising money, you know these email scams. And tourists are often an easy target for robbers and muggers.

Chris: That's a reason for me not to travel to some countries. I really don't want to seem like a king in a five-star hotel when there are people who are hungry next door.

Tony: It's actually better to work or study in another country anyway (10) *then / than* to go as a tourist. Students often spend a term or do an internship abroad so they can get to know the country.

Helen: That is a really good thing about education nowadays, learning about other countries and customs. It is a pity communication is always in English (11) *so / though*!

Chris: What do you mean – a pity? Life is much easier if we all speak the same language!

Helen: I don't agree at all …

2c **What will the future be? Use your notebook and write down sentences. More than one option is possible.**

Growing organic food Speaking more than one language People	will	become be eat	less prepared food. more important. big business.

3 **How well do you know the *Extra Practice* sections? Use your notebook and write down the questions. Then look at each unit and find the answers.**

Extra Practice Unit 1: at the North Cape? / does / do / Eva / in the long winters / What

What does Eva do in the long winters at the North Cape? She knits pullovers for the tourists who want a souvenir.

Extra Practice Unit 2: from Facebook? / Lisa and Janine / did / their new friends / in order to meet / go / Where

Extra Practice Unit 3: Juan's / did / Where / business partner / for dinner? / invite him

Extra Practice Unit 4: can / What / eat / Helly / every day?

Extra Practice Unit 5: Susanne / did / How much money / have / to Italy? / for her first trip

Extra Practice Unit 6: does / Which trend / the picture / show? / in exercise 6.2

Extra Practice Unit 7: in Australia? / of the traditional instrument / is the name / played / by the Aborigines / What

Extra Practice Unit 8: What / Anna's / was / called? / non-alcoholic drink

Extra Practice Unit 9: would / What / do / Betty and Dorothy / if they won / at the bingo hall? / £10,000

Extra Practice Unit 10: does / What / on? / Sam / live

Extra Practice Unit 11: Why / in her life? / only once / fly / Marianne / did

Extra Practice Unit 12: on TV / like to watch / Naomi / did / What / when she was a teenager?

4 **Who is your favourite person in all the units? Write a short description of the person on a piece of paper, but don't write the name of the person. Bring your paper to class and show it to some other students. Can they guess who the person is?**

DOING BUSINESS IN DIFFERENT CULTURES

Not long ago, a colleague told me about the German engineer, Michael Schmidt, who went to England on business for the first time. He introduced himself in England with the words "Good morning, my name is Schmidt." Everyone looked surprised and then someone asked him "Can you tell us your first name?" Herr Schmidt answered with this question: "Why do you want to know that?" Not everyone knows that in the UK it is very common to use first names quickly, especially if you are all at the same level in the business.

First meetings are always very important because as the saying goes "You only have one chance to make a first impression". How do you introduce yourself? The best thing is probably to use both names. You can also say what you would like people to call you "My name is Ulrike Leopold. Please call me Uli." Do you shake hands? This is the usual thing to do in business these days but in some countries, like India, women do not shake hands with other women or with men. The Japanese bow when they meet for the first time, but they don't always expect foreigners to do it.

Then there is the question of what you do first. Is there a lot of small talk before business starts? Many people say Germans are no good at small talk. Some Germans say this too, but it is not true.

Maybe Germans do things in a different order (business first and then small talk) but everyone, even Germans, can talk about the weather, the place they are in and ask questions about a flight and the weather at home. Small talk is important and it is helpful to know when it takes place and how long it should go on for. In some countries there is a lot of small talk and it seems the business is not very important. What can you do? Should you be patient or try and get down to business quickly? Sometimes business is over very quickly. What does this mean?

Karl, a successful German businessman, now in his forties remembers his first business trip to New York. His American colleague gave him coffee in a paper cup and asked him two questions: "How much discount can you offer us?" and "What marketing will you do?" There was no small talk and the negotiation was over in fifteen minutes, leaving Karl plenty of time to go sightseeing in New York. Karl has now done business all over the world and knows that things are very different in different countries. He also knows you cannot be prepared for everything.

In some countries there is a lot of eating and drinking before or after the business. What do you do if you are offered something to eat which seems strange, like fish eyes? Can you refuse and say you would prefer another dish? Do you want to drink a lot of alcohol if you have to work the next day? Can you eat with chopsticks?

And there is more – socialising in general, dress code, what gifts to give and accept. The list is almost endless. Everything can be what you expect or completely different when you do business with other people!

Here are some golden rules for working with people from other countries:

- Always be polite. It doesn't matter if you make mistakes when you speak English as long as you don't offend or confuse people.
- Accept that things are different in different places. This can mean different clothes, different food and different customs and manners.
- Find out as much as possible about the country, the culture, the company and the people.
- Remember that things can always go wrong. You cannot be prepared for everything but you can try to make things as easy as possible for you and your business partners if and when things go wrong.

The future

If I could change something about my job, I would …
I want to improve my English for / to …
Email will be more important in the future.
Text messaging will be less important.
I would like to try …
Soon we won't need any …
Nowadays it is impossible to …
How has your English changed?
I'm definitely going to …

Writing emails

Dear …
With best wishes
All the best
I'm afraid I can't …
I'd love to …
Thank you very much for …
I am writing to …
I would like you to …
Could you possibly …?

Negotiating

Can you give me a discount?
I'd prefer a …
I really want to …
I can offer you …
I'm afraid that is not possible.
I would like to suggest …

Talking about travel and work

What do you do?
I could be a … because I …
Work is meaningful / pleasant / useful …
It is good to have a routine.
I would like to work as a …
I never … at work.
Travelling for work is …
I sometimes get fed up with …
The flight was cancelled.
I had to stay an extra night.
The hotel is dirty / cold …

My useful expression corner

USEFUL EXPRESSIONS

I got my first … when I was …
Email is more important than Twitter.
I have never …
This happened to me only …
If you want other people to understand you, you should …
English is becoming more …
English is an official language in …
I hate …
I would never …

Add some other useful expressions from Module 4 that you want to remember.

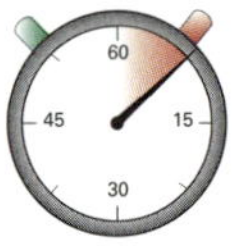

Look back at what you have done in Module 4 and prepare a one-minute talk about work. Talk about what it is, how you feel about it, your personal experience and any other details.

Read the following checklist and tick a smiley.

Now I can …	☺	😐	☹
… say how I feel about work.			
… say what I would do if something changed in my life.			
… describe what people do as part of their work.			
… give reasons why I would be good at something.			
… give information about where English is spoken.			
… understand people with different accents speaking English.			
… understand short emails.			
… write a short email in reply to a request.			
… talk about the advantages and disadvantages of travelling for work.			
… write an email complaining about something.			
… understand people making simple negotiations.			
… use phrases to negotiate something.			
… understand texts about the use of English today.			
… talk about my plans for the future.			
… talk about organizing a reunion.			

Think about the following questions and discuss them with a partner.

What was new for you? What did you remember? What would you like to do better? What was the most difficult thing to learn?

Files

UNIT 7

1c Student A

Explain the first word to your partner without saying the word. Then listen to your partner.

mobile phone

adult

wardrobe

vegetables

ice cream

Now find three more words from the last units and go on with the activity.

UNIT 7

4e Student A

Read the following text to your partner. Make sure that you just mumble the underlined words so that your partner can't understand you. Your partner will ask you to explain. Then your partner will read a similar text to you. Use the phrases from 4e to ask questions.

The Indians have lots of <u>problems</u>. And almost all of them have to do with <u>land</u>. Today, their land is still taken over for ranches and industrial projects. A lot of new <u>farms</u> and ranches need huge areas of land. And there is a massive <u>boom</u> in oil and gas exploration, illegal cutting down of expensive <u>trees</u>, etc.

1c Student B

Listen to your partner and find out the word. Then give your partner an explanation without saying the word.

grandmother

CD

padlock

farm

mountains

Now find three more words from the last units and go on with the activity.

UNIT 7

4e Student B

Your partner is going to read a short text to you. There will be words which you can hardly understand. Ask your partner to explain. Use the phrases in 4e. Then read your text to your partner. Make sure that you just mumble the underlined words so that your partner will not understand you and ask you to explain.

Today, most Indians in the Amazon have access to western healthcare and education. When these are controlled by the Indians themselves they are usually very successful. And don't forget: Amazon Indians have given the world a lot of knowledge of totally unknown plants and their medical benefits!

Language overview

This is a general overview. It contains • the most important grammar and its use at this level (B1). There is no repetition of very basic grammar; • the most common ways in which the grammatical forms are used, mainly in speaki"ng but also in texts; • authentic examples of how language is used; • other useful language examples; • tips for using language.

All the examples are from the *Units* and the *Extra Practice*, so you can see how language works in real life. The numbers in brackets refer to the *Unit* the example is taken from. If you want to know more details or find out more about the basics of the grammar described, we recommend you use one of the many grammar books available. Remember grammar is only useful for communication. There is no need to know the rules of grammar. It is important to use language to communicate well and correctly!

1 Verbs and Tenses

1.1 Present simple

The present simple is usually formed from the infinitive. An *s* is added for the 3rd person singular (*he, she* and *it*). It is the most basic form and is used often when talking about facts and repeated actions.

I work in … (1)
I feel a bit shy when speaking English. (1)
I look after the children of my aupair family. (1)
Juliet work**s** only to earn money. (10)

It is used with *sometimes, always, never, often* and similar words.

They **sometimes** have difficulties at the beginning because the new partner and the children do not **always** get on well. (2)

Questions are formed with *do* or *does* + the subject + the infinitive.

What **do** you do? (1, 10)
What languages **do** they speak? (1)
How many offices **does** Lonemoney have? (4)

Try to remember the s for *he*, *she* and *it*.

Negatives are formed with *don't* or *doesn't* + the infinitive.

What do you do with things you **don't** want? (4)

1.2 Present continuous

The present continuous is formed with the present tense of *to be* + the *-ing* form of the verb.
It is used to describe things happening or continuing at the moment.

Hello, this **is** … speak**ing**. (6)
I **am** writ**ing** to … (10)

The present continuous is not used for the present as often as the present simple. If you are not sure, use the present simple.

It is used for actions or events happening only for a short time.

We **are** look**ing** for an aupair. (1)

It is used for future events.

I don't think I **am** go**ing** to Yoga today. (11)
I'**m** gett**ing** a … next month. (12)

It is used for trends.

Freshly Farmed **is** becom**ing** a popular alternative. (6)

1.3 Past simple

The past simple is formed by adding *-ed* to the infinitive with regular verbs. A list of irregular verbs can be found in this book (p. 105). The past simple is used for specific past actions (often the time is given). It is also used when it is clear that the event or action is over. It is used more often than the present perfect.

When I was a child, I lov**ed** eating noodles with ketchup. (3)
I **went** to school in … (1)
It **became** clear I had to learn English. (1)
Two weeks ago I **bought** some vegetables at my local supermarket. (6)
I **was** born in … (1)

Questions are formed with *did* + the subject + the infinitive.
Did you know? (2)
How **did** he get a fridge? (4)

Negatives are formed with *didn't* + the infinitive.
When I was in school we **didn't** use computers at all. (12)

> If you are not sure which tense to use when talking about the past, use the simple past.

1.4 Present perfect

The present perfect is formed with *has* or *have* + the infinitive + *-ed* with regular verbs. A list of irregular verbs can be found in this book (p. 105). The present perfect is used to describe something which started in the past and is still going on.

> The present perfect is used with words like *how long, ever, never, since, for*.
> As soon as you give details, use the simple past.

They **have had** contact with outsiders for almost 500 years. (7)

It is used to describe things you have always or never done.
Have you ever work**ed** as an aupair? (1)
I **have been** to the jungle several times. (7)
I **have** always **been** fascinated by ... (9)
How long **have** you **had** this old-fashioned pair of glasses? (9)

It is used when no specific time is given.
How often **have** you **been** to Australia? (7)

> Don't overuse the present perfect when talking about the past. If you are not sure, use the simple past.

1.5 Present perfect continuous

The present perfect continuous is formed with *has* or *have been* + the *-ing* form.
It is used for actions, activities and events which started in the past and are still continuing.
… and now I **have been** liv**ing** in Berlin for twenty years. (1)

1.6 *Used to …*

This is formed with *used to* + the infinitive.
It is used for actions in the past which are over.
Susan never **used to check** where the food was grown. (6)

> Be careful when using this form. It is only used for things you do not do any more!

1.7 *Will* Future

This is formed with *will* + the infinitive. It is used if the future event or action is not certain, often with *I think …, I hope …*
I think the text **will be** about … (7)
Soon we **won't need** money any more. (12)

> *Will* is used when you are not quite sure if something will happen.

It is used for promises, offers and spontaneous decisions.
We **will** never **bomb** your country. (2)
We **will contact** you if the position becomes vacant. (11)

1.8 *Going to* Future

This is formed with *going to* + the infinitive.
It is used for plans and intentions.
I am definitely **going to do** another English course. (12)

> The present continuous is used most often for talking about the future.

1.9 Passive

This is formed with *to be* in the appropriate tense + the past form (perfect).
It is used when the person doing the action is not important or not known.
When **was** the first carrier pigeon **used**? (8)
The first email **was written** in 1971. (8)

It is used when the person or people doing the action are not as important as the action.
A hundred different languages **are spoken** here. (10)

> If you know who did something, the passive is not always necessary.

It is often used in writing.

1.10 Conditionals

These are sentences with *if*. Conditionals are used for talking about future events.
You can stay till midnight if I pick you up. (10)
If you … then I will … (10)

They are used for talking about possibilities.
If I could live my life again, I would change almost nothing. (3)
What would you buy with €10? (4)
You could grow vegetables in your garden. (4)
If we won €10,000 we would buy a lot of wool. (9)
I wish I could give up my job. (10)

> Depending on the meaning, these can be mixed. Don't worry too much about the rules!

1.11 Imperative

This is formed by the infinitive. It is used for instructions and for formal, impersonal advice.
Use your notebook and put the information into two groups. (2)
Don't spend your money before you earn it. (4)

> Don't use the imperative to ask someone to do something or to suggest something! This can sound rude.

1.12 Modals *(can, must, should, may, might)*

These are formed with the appropriate verb and the infinitive.
They are used to show opinions, feelings and possibilities and for giving advice.
Patchwork families **can** be very happy. (2)
You **can't** eat it. (4)
The summers in Denmark **must** be colder than German summers. (3)
What **should** you do if you find €100 on the street? (5)
You **may** only have one alcoholic drink in front of you at a time. (5)
It **might** have been in 1998. (8)

> *May* and *might* mean the same.

1.13 *Have to* and *must*

Have to and *must* are used to show that something is necessary.
Don't have to means something is not necessary.

I **had to** pay a fine. (5)
All men driving motorcycles **must** wear shirts. (5)

Must not means that something is not allowed or forbidden.
You must not open an umbrella on a street if a horse is near. (5)

> Don't use *must not* when you mean something is not necessary but can be done. *Must not* means that something is not allowed!

1.14 *Have something done*

This is formed with the correct tense of *have* + the noun + the past form of the verb.
It is used when you don't do something yourself but ask and (usually) pay someone to do it.

You should **have** your ears **checked**. (9)

> Don't use *let*. That means something completely different. Be careful with the order of the words.

1.15 Verb + *-ing*

The *-ing* form is used with some verbs, e.g. *like, love, hate, enjoy, be keen on, be interested in*.

I like go**ing** to the cinema. (2)
I wouldn't like to be a chambermaid because I hate clean**ing**. (10)

> Sometimes the verb + *to* can be used (*I like to go the cinema* = *I like going to the cinema*) but the verb + *-ing* form is more common and more often correct.

It is used when actions are used like nouns (e.g. *I like cakes / I like eating cakes*).

What are the pros and cons of liv**ing** without money? (4)
Travell**ing** without a ticket is wrong. (5)
What is a good punishment for cheat**ing**? (5)
What do you think about play**ing** the piano at midday? (5)

1.16 Multi-part verbs

There are many verbs which are used with other words and change their meaning a bit. *Look* and *take* are two examples.

Look after means *take care of*, *look for* means *search for* and *look forward to* is how you feel about something nice in the future.

You need to **look after** someone else's kids. (1)
We are **looking for** an aupair. (1)
I hope you are fine and **looking forward** to Christmas! (3)

Take part in means *do something with others* and *take place* means *happen*.

2,130 adults from England, Wales and Scotland **took part** in the survey. (8)
It seems that 80% of all business conversations in English now **take place** without any native speakers present. (10)

1.17 *Make* and *let*

Make means *force* and *let* means *allow*.

Money **makes** the world go round. (4)

My parents **made** me do my homework every day. (8)

My grandpa **let** me use his boat in the holidays. (8)

Don't mix up *make* and *let*!

1.18 *Think* and *mean*

There are several ways of giving your opinion. For example, you can say *I think, I feel* or *I believe*. *I mean* is used when you explain something in more detail.

I think the same. (2)

What does this **mean** for English learners? (10)

The easiest way to give your opinion is to say *I think* …

2 Adjectives and adverbs

2.1 Comparatives and superlatives

These are usually formed by adding *-er* and *-est* to the adjective. For adjectives of more than two syllables, *more* and *most* are used.

The cheap**est** newspaper is just under … (4)

What was the **most** interesting piece of information you heard? (1)

Who are the happ**iest** people in the world? (3)

The weather in Spain is **better** than the weather in Germany. (3)

Which saying do you like **least**? (4)

Sack gardens will be **more** important in the future. (12)

Remember: *good, better, best*
bad, worse, worst
little, less, least

2.2 Adverbs

These are used to describe actions in more detail.

I **slightly** disagree

I **strongly** agree.

Don't worry too much about these as not all native speakers use them correctly all the time!

3 Numbers and amounts

3.1 Numbers

Decimal points are used for parts of a number and commas for talking about numbers over one thousand.

One point five litres of milk. (4)

This is important especially if talking and writing about money, so make sure you get it right!

3.2 *Much* and *many*

Many is used for things which can be counted and *much* for amounts which cannot be counted.

I have too **many** books. (4)

I have too **much** food in my fridge. (4)

This is the same as in German.

4 Pronouns

4.1 *Which*, *who* and *that*

Which is used when talking about things,
who is used when talking about people.
That can be used for both.

Use *that* if you can't remember.

Someone **who** you see sometimes is an acquaintance. (2)
My opinion of social networks is **that** they are … (2)
A loan is money **that** you borrow from a bank. (4)
It's a person **who** … (7)
It's a thing **which** … (7)

4.2 *This* and *these*

This is used for one thing and *these* for several things. Usually the things you are talking about are near you or important. If they are further away or less important, you can say *that* and *those*. All the words are used when you mean something special.

This way, they can make a loan on the same day. (4)
You use **these** machines in places where you don't normally have access to electrical power from the grid. (7)

5 Questions

Common question words are *how*, *what*, *where*, *why*, *who*, and *when*.
How means *In what way …?*
Where is used to ask about a place,
why is used when you want a reason for something,
who to ask about a person and
when to ask about a time.

How does he get food? (4)
What's your name? (1)
Where do you live? (1)
Why do pupils cheat in tests at school? (5)
Who are the happiest people in the world? (3)
When do you have to pay it back? (4)

6 Nouns

6.1. Words for relatives

Some examples of men (male) family members are:

father	nephew	stepfather
husband	father-in-law	boyfriend
brother	grandfather	

Some examples of women (female) family members are:

mother	niece	stepmother
wife	mother-in-law	girlfriend
sister	grandmother	

6.2. Opposites

Not all words have an opposite but some can be easily confused.

Borrow means *to take something from someone for a time*.

Lend means *to give something to someone for a time*.

How much can you **borrow** if you have twelve bottles of a Chateau Petrus? (4)

Banks and companies accept wine jewels and art in return for **lending** money. (4)

Some other opposites are:

forget	⇔	remember	true	⇔	false	sell	⇔	buy
more	⇔	less	slow	⇔	fast	live	⇔	die
short	⇔	long	big	⇔	small	cheap	⇔	expensive
love	⇔	hate	find	⇔	lose	black	⇔	white

LANGUAGE OVERVIEW

List of irregular verbs

infinitive	past simple	past participle	infinitive	past simple	past participle
be	was / were	been	leave	left	left
become	became	become	lend	lent	lent
begin	began	begun	let	let	let
blow	blew	blown	lie	lay	lain
break	broke	broken	lose	lost	lost
bring	brought	brought	make	made	made
build	built	built	mean	meant	meant
buy	bought	bought	meet	met	met
catch	caught	caught	misunderstand	misunderstood	misunderstood
choose	chose	chosen	pay	paid	paid
come	came	come	put	put	put
cost	cost	cost	quit	quit	quit
cut	cut	cut	read	read	read
do	did	done	ring	rang	rung
draw	drew	drawn	run	ran	run
dream	dreamt	dreamt	say	said	said
drink	drank	drunk	see	saw	seen
drive	drove	driven	sell	sold	sold
eat	ate	eaten	send	sent	sent
fall	fell	fallen	set	set	set
feel	felt	felt	shake	shook	shaken
fight	fought	fought	shine	shone	shone
find	found	found	shoot	shot	shot
fly	flew	flown	show	showed	shown
forbid	fobade	forbidden	sit	sat	sat
forget	forgot	forgotten	sleep	slept	slept
get	got	got	speak	spoke	spoken
give	gave	given	spend	spent	spent
go	went	gone	stand	stood	stood
grow	grew	grown	steal	stole	stolen
hang	hung	hung	swear	swore	sworn
have	had	had	take	took	taken
hear	heard	heard	teach	taught	taught
hide	hid	hidden	tell	told	told
hit	hit	hit	think	thought	thought
hold	held	held	throw	threw	thrown
keep	kept	kept	understand	understood	understood
knit	knit / knitted	knit / knitted	wake up	woke up	woken up
know	knew	known	wear	wore	worn
lead	led	led	win	won	won
learn	learnt, learned	learnt, learned	write	wrote	written

Tapescripts

Module 1 You and me

Unit 1 A new start

1

2a

Monika: My name's Monika. I was born in Hungary, and when I went to kindergarten I learnt to speak German. That was great fun! We sang songs and played a lot. I really enjoyed that ... Then I learnt to play the guitar, and I liked the Beatles' songs best. So it became clear that I needed to learn English – I wanted to understand the lyrics! We moved to Germany when I was fifteen, and now I'm married with two kids. Next year Sina will go to school and Tim will start kindergarten, so I think I'd like to start work again, and brushing up my English gives me a good feeling for a fresh start in my job.

Madhu: Hi there! My name is Madhu. I was born in India, in Delhi, and of course I speak Hindi. At school we learnt English, but I wasn't very good at that because we mostly read stories or listened to our teacher. We never really spoke much. When I was nine my family moved to Spain because my father is an actor and he was invited to make several films there. I learnt Spanish quickly because I had a lot of friends in Barcelona. After a few years we moved again, and now I have been living in Berlin for twenty years. My daughter is planning to go to California for a year as an au pair, and all the application forms are in English. So I think it is a good idea for me to brush up my English! And I'm looking forward to making new friends in the English course!

Sebastian: My name's Sebastian, but everybody calls me Seb. I was born in Meersburg, a small town on Lake Constance. At school I liked maths and physics, but foreign languages were not really my cup of tea. I am an engineer now. Well, to be honest, I feel a bit shy when it comes to speaking English. Reading and understanding is not a big problem, but talking to others is more difficult for me. And the worst thing is making phone calls with English-speaking customers! I hope I'll be able to deal with these situations better at the end of this course!

2

2d

1. I was born in Hungary, and when I went to kindergarten I learnt to speak German.
2. So it became clear that I needed to learn English.
3. I learnt Spanish quickly because I had a lot of friends in Barcelona.
4. After a few years we moved again, and now I have been living in Berlin for twenty years.
5. I am an engineer now. Well, to be honest, I feel a bit shy when it comes to speaking English.

Unit 2 Family & friends

3

3d

Speaker 1

Facebook's great. People are naturally social and they love information. The best kind of information is about people they know, their friends. And Facebook is a site where you can be with friends. It's a kind of place to hang out online. Also people don't go there just once or twice a day; they go dozens of times every single day, just to look at the people they know there. You can find out who's going out with who and what new news is out. That's why it's so successful.

Speaker 2

I think Facebook is so successful because people are for the most part sheep and cattle, you know cows always follow each other like sheep. Well, people like feeling they are connected to the "herd", the group, and like feeling important when they post something on Facebook, even though 99% of the garbage on Facebook is a complete waste of time and energy.

Speaker 3
I can't tell you why it is successful. I'm not on it, but as a business idea it's interesting. The big question, of course, is what is Facebook worth? It's not only interesting because so many people use Facebook, but because it went public at a really high price. Since Facebook is free to use, it has to make money from its customers and advertisers. It must do that, I suppose.

Speaker 4
Facebook is fine for people under about thirty-five, but that's it, in my opinion. I don't believe that grandparents should use it. And also married people don't realise the dangers of getting in touch with old boyfriends and girlfriends. It can damage a relationship. Also a lot of older people don't understand the privacy settings or the danger of viruses. It's not really so easy to use but people feel it is and I suppose that's why it's a success.

Unit 2 - Extra practice

4

2a

See track 3.

Unit 3 Love and happiness

5

4d

Radio presenter: ... now this is Radio Starlight, and welcome to our afternoon programme of "Your turn!" As you know we have a different topic every day, and you just phone in and let us know your story. Today's topic is "What made and makes you happy?", and I can see the first call coming in! Hello, this is Radio Starlight, I'm John ...

Eri: Hello, my name's Eri. I'm Japanese, and in our culture happiness means love and family, but also a good career and financial security. When I was a child we moved to Berlin, and I was very happy when I was allowed to watch Japanese TV because I was homesick. What I do to keep happy? Every morning, when I wake up, I think to myself: Wow! Another day! Welcome! And then I try and enjoy the day.

Juan: Hi there! I'm Juan from Mexico, and in my childhood the greatest moments were – my birthdays! I loved the presents, I loved the parties – and I was allowed to eat as much ice cream as I wanted! That was great. Now I have a family of my own, and my tip for you is, meet your friends and family as often as you can. You are never happier than when you're loved!

Sabrina: Good afternoon! I'm Sabrina from London. When I was a child I used to play a lot with kids from the neighbourhood. We spent most afternoons on a playground nearby and I really enjoyed that. But I can remember very well that later on in my life I used to think a fantastic career with an enormous salary would make me really happy. Well, I must admit I enjoyed that time – business trips around the world, and my name in the newspapers. Now I'm retired, and I have found out that I'm even happier now that I'm doing voluntary work for the local Oxfam shop – and I earn nothing but smiles and happiness!

Unit 3 - Extra practice

6

3

See track 5, Juan.

Module 2 The world around us

Unit 4 Money

7

2a

1,456 – 1,500,000 – 26 – 3.25 – 43,000 – 750,000 – 8.83

8

5c

Radio presenter: Our next feature is about Andrew Woodruffe, who has found a new way of living. He and his girlfriend and daughter seem like a normal family, but there is one difference. They live without spending any money. This means they also don't borrow or lend money. I'm sure listeners will be asking "How do they do it? Are they healthy?" Andrew, tell us how you live.

Andrew: Well of course we need food just like other people. We don't work so we have plenty of time and can go to skips in the evening and get the food which shops throw away. It is really unbelievable how much food is wasted every day. Most of it is perfectly good and there is so much that we can choose what we want. It is not old or bad and it is all packed. We drink milk and eat milk products as often as we want and our daughter Helly can eat spaghetti every day like other children. There is always much more than we need.

Radio presenter: But what about fresh food, fruit and vegetables and so on? And do you eat meat?

Andrew: No, we are all vegetarians, actually, but we eat lots of fruit and vegetables. I love growing my own and Helly is keen on gardening too. We eat what is in season and it costs nothing. We freeze what we can't eat immediately.

Radio presenter: And how did you get a freezer and a fridge? They usually cost money.

Andrew: Most people have too many things and they want new things before they need them and that goes for our friends too. Friends give us their old things. That means we also have a television and a radio and a computer. We could have much more if we wanted but we don't. We have as many clothes and shoes as we need and get those from our friends too.

Radio presenter: Andrew, you don't spend money. But do you earn money?

Andrew: I don't go to work, but Julie, my partner does. We live in our own house and we pay for electricity and gas and water. But we try not to spend anything else.

Radio presenter: That is probably the answer many listeners wanted to hear. I'm sure our listeners have many more questions, but time is running out so my last question is an easy one. How do you travel?

Andrew: And the answer is easy too. On foot or by bike of course!

Unit 4 – Extra practice

9

3

See track 8.

Unit 5 Crime and punishment

10

1e

You know, there are many reasons why pupils cheat and are dishonest: pressure from the parents, heavy workload, too many tests on one day, and so forth. But we must all make sure that pupils know that cheating at school is wrong. In fact, we must encourage them to be honest. If we catch a pupil cheating, he or she will be punished. We walk around the class in tests. If pupils have cheat sheets or notes, they will fail the test. If they are punished, they will learn that there is no reason to cheat.

Unit 6 Does it matter?

11

1b

You know, something strange happened to me lately. I was shopping at the supermarket as usual. I bought all sorts of things, and especially a lot of vegetables because I wanted to make a ratatouille for my friends, you know, courgettes, aubergines, tomatoes, garlic, the lot. I mean I always buy things in the supermarket, I don't have much time to go from small shop to small shop, so the supermarket is the most convenient place for my shopping. When

I came home I unpacked my stuff, and just like that and for no special reason, I glanced at the little label on the garlic, and I read "Garlic from Argentina". What? Argentina? I just couldn't believe my eyes!

garlic from
ust a
by

Imagine the transport costs, the fuel for the plane or the freight ships, the air pollution just for my three bulbs of garlic!! Now, who's stupid: me, the consumer, or the supermarket owners? I suddenly knew I had to change something, and I did.

Unit 6 – Extra practice

13

4

See track 11.

Module 3 Changes

Unit 7 Global changes

14

4c

Interviewer: Hi Laura, nice to have you with us here today. In this broadcast we're talking to people who bring some sort of change into the world. Where do you think there will be change?

Laura: Well, thank you for inviting me, and yes, I think there will be some massive change in the Amazon area soon.

Interviewer: In the Amazon area? You mean in Brazil?

Laura: Yes, that's right. In Brazil – and in quite a few other countries – there are a lot of people living without the benefits of energy, that is, they have no access to a regular supply of electrical power.

Interviewer: What exactly does this mean?

Laura: The Amazon Indians of Brazil live in small villages, mostly no more than 20 families per village, and they live far away from civilization, so they have no electrical power. This means they live without lamps, without cookers, without radio, without television. And we're talking about more than one million people!

Interviewer: So what you are saying is that one million people in Brazil live in the rainforest with no contact to the outside world?

Laura: Not really. Many tribes use gensets to create electrical power.

Interviewer: Sorry? I didn't really get that. Gensets? What are they?

15

4f

Laura: A genset is a generator powered by fuel or gas, and it creates electrical power. You use these machines in places where you don't normally have access to electrical power from the grid. For example, in far-away islands, or when you build roads or new buildings, you need gensets. And you have emergency gensets in modern hospitals and hotels, just in case of a power shortage.

Interviewer: Okay ... But you said they need fuel? Where does it come from?

Laura: That's a good question. Most Indian tribes need a 3-day-trip to get some fuel. First they walk through the jungle to the nearest river, then they paddle their canoes up or down the Amazon to buy fuel in some small town, and finally they paddle and carry huge cans with fuel back home.

Interviewer: Phew ... that doesn't sound very convenient.

Laura: No, definitely not.

Interviewer: So what will change now?

Laura: Solar energy is the solution. Modern systems can stand alone wherever they are needed in the world, and they produce energy without any trouble.

Unit 7 – Extra practice

16

2a

See track 14.

17

2b

See track 15.

Unit 8 (Dis)Connected?

18

3c

Dad: Look what I found on the Internet this morning. It's an advertisement for a holiday in a black hole resort.

Mum: I don't want to leave this planet. You never know what you might find in other galaxies.

Dad: No, look, a black hole resort is a hotel where they block off all incoming and outgoing signals, so no Internet, no TV, no mobile phones. It sounds like heaven to me.

Anna: You're kidding, dad, aren't you?

Dad: No, I'm serious, really. I can't imagine anything better than two weeks of beach life and sunshine and my family around and nothing else!

Anna: A nightmare! Mum, can I stay at home?

Mum: You're too young to stay at home alone, dear, and besides, we would love to spend a holiday together.

Anna: OK, but you can't make me leave my mobile phone at home! What about my friends? I need to know what's going on! And what about my music? And I wouldn't even know what time it is without my mobile!

Dad: Well, I guess you don't need to know the time when you are on holiday. You get up with the sunrise ...

Anna: ... and go to bed when the sun sets. I can't believe it. I'm sixteen, not sixty-one!

Mum: Well, it's in Mexico, isn't it? There will probably be a lot of activities to do there, like windsurfing, yoga, riding on the beach ...

Anna: Riding on the beach? Wow! That sounds good? I must text Sandra ...

Dad: I think I'd like to try kite surfing. And you?

Mum: Is lying in a deckchair an activity?

Dad: Of course ...

Mum: Then just watch me be active all day long ...

Anna: Would you let me try diving? They say that they have fantastic coral reefs there ...

Mum: Sure, why not?

Anna: But what if a tsunami comes? We wouldn't even know because we won't have a TV ...

Mum and Dad: Uaarrggghh ...

Unit 8 – Extra practice

19

2a

See track 18.

Unit 9 Unusual hobbies

20

2a

Betty: Hello Dorothy. How are you today?

Dorothy: I'm fine, love. And you?

Betty: Well, my back aches as usual, but otherwise I'm fine. What are you doing?

Dorothy: I'm doing guerrilla knitting.

Betty: What? Do you really think it's very cold at the zoo?

Dorothy: Oh, noooo ... Listen, dear, you don't only have problems with your back, you should have your ears checked! Guerilla! G-U-E-R-I-L-L-A! Not gorilla!

Betty: Guerilla knitting? What is that? It sounds very dangerous ...

21

2b

Dorothy: Now look out of the window, Betty. Don't you agree it's a really depressing view? How often have we asked the mayor to make our town more beautiful? There are so many derelict industrial buildings, no parks, no colours – it's awful, isn't it?

Betty: You're right, and they always say they have no money to make our town more attractive ...

Dorothy: That's it! I'm sick and tired of this hopeless grey town! So I'm knitting a colourful cosy for the lamppost over there, and Margret is knitting a green and yellow cosy for the bridge railing, and ...

Betty: ... and the mayor agreed to that?

Dorothy: Of course not. Actually, it is not quite legal, just like painting graffiti on buildings is illegal, however ugly the buildings are ...

Betty: Dorothy, I'm not sure. You used to knit socks for your grandchildren, and now you are on the road to prison! On the other hand, it sounds rather exciting ... I think I like the idea. Have you got any wool left? ...

Unit 9 - ʼ

22

3a

See tracks 20 and 21.

Module 4 Work

Unit 10 Jobs and languages

23

1b

1

Hi, my name's Charlotte. I have worked in marketing since I left university and last year my partner and I decided to give up our jobs and travel around South America for a year. We saved money for the trip and when we were in South America we worked a little bit, teaching English. The experience changed my ideas about work and now we are working only to earn money for our next trip which will be to Asia! I can imagine doing this for the next twenty years, as long as we can find jobs. At the moment we are working in London in a hotel as a room maid and a waiter. We can live and eat there, too, so we can save a lot of money.

2

Hi, I'm Juliet. I have a wonderful job which I enjoy, but if I could retire tomorrow, I would. I do interesting work, earn a good salary, have a great boss and very pleasant colleagues and have flexible working hours and a home office so I can work more or less when I want. Of course I need the money but there are so many other things I would like to do with my time, like reading, talking to friends, cooking and visiting places.

3

Hi, my name's Sam. I inherited some houses from my grandfather and can live on the rent which I get from them so I don't need to work. Of course, it is nice having enough money to live on without working but I have to find meaningful things to do with my time. I can draw very well so I draw pictures for children's books which is fun and I can do it whenever I want. My wife and I go on holiday a lot and I like working in the house and garden, not cleaning and so on, but designing and decorating. That's enough work for me.

4

I'm David. I work as a freelance translator and only work when I need to. I live alone in a small flat and don't have a high standard of living so I often refuse work if I don't need the money. I enjoy the freedom my work gives me and so I usually only work about twenty-five hours a week. That's enough for me. Some of my friends don't understand it, but for me money is not everything. I enjoy the other things in life too much.

24

3d

My name's Seiko. I was very good at English at school but we never had to speak much so I am nervous about speaking now. I can write everything I want to communicate! When I write English, people say my English is very good, but when I speak I think I am difficult to understand because of my Japanese accent. I want to get a better accent. I often have to go to meetings which are in English and I am shy about saying anything there.

Hi, I'm Olga. I don't think my English is very good because I only have a basic vocabulary. I use English a lot for my work because I travel to branches of our company abroad and help with software problems. That's my job. The branches are in many countries and not all my colleagues speak good English but it is the language we have in common, our company language. People find me easy to understand because my English is simple! I don't know if that is a compliment or not! Well, I definitely need to learn more words and improve my vocabulary.

My name's Fabian. I think my accent is quite good because I spent a year working in America and I am usually easy to understand for most people. But I still make grammar mistakes and nobody corrects me. Native speakers say grammar doesn't matter, but I think it is important. I just never have time to do grammar exercises.

Unit 10 – Extra practice

25

2

See track 23, Charlotte.

26

3a

See track 23, Juliet, David und Sam.

Unit 11 Work and communication

27

3a

Ralph: Hi, my name's Ralph. I'm a pilot, so my job is travelling so I couldn't do it if I didn't like travelling. I love flying but only if I am in charge of the plane and definitely not as a passenger. I have been flying long haul flights for ten years now and have seen very many interesting places. It's great to visit somewhere like Delhi in India for a few days and then return as a tourist with my wife. I think I have the perfect job as I can plan my holidays as part of my work. The only disadvantage is that when I travel on holiday, I have to be a passenger on a plane!

Marianne: I'm Marianne. I don't like flying and would hate to travel for my work. I have only flown once because we wanted to visit my daughter in America and I was really scared. So travelling far away is not for me. I'm a real home lover and my work as a checkout assistant at a supermarket in my village suits me fine. I can walk to work and walk home for lunch and I meet lots of people every day. That's all I want from work.

Dieter: Hi, my name's Dieter. My job is Head of Facilities and I look after the technical side of things in the company and sometimes I drive the boss to meetings in different parts of the country. I'm not really a chauffeur but as I really enjoy driving, I think it might be a good job to have. I can listen to music in the car as my boss usually wants to work or is on the phone during the journey and when he is in the meeting, I can go for a walk or have a cup of coffee in a café I see different parts of the country and that's fine for me.

Vicki: Hi, I'm Vicki. I never thought writing a book could mean so much travelling. A year ago, I wrote a best-seller about a young mother and now I travel around and read from my book. I stay in some really strange places, sometimes in hotels and sometimes in people's homes, but it is all very interesting. I'm usually only away from home for a night so my family can manage without me and I can bring my children nice presents. I'm not sure if I want to travel more but my book is being translated into other languages so maybe I will have to!

28

4b

1

Chris: Hey, Mum, can I stay out until midnight on Saturday? It's Philip's birthday, you know.

Pamela: Midnight? That is really too late. You know what we said, nine on weekdays and ten on Saturdays. You're only thirteen.

Chris: Everyone else can stay later than ten. I'm not a baby!

Pamela: Well, how are you going to get home? Dad and I don't want to come out at that time.

Chris: Jack's dad said he will bring us home but Jack can stay out later than ten. I'd really like to stay there as late as the others. Please ...

Pamela: I'll have to think about it. How long can Jack stay at the party?

Chris: I think until about eleven. Later than ten I know!

Pamela: Well, we could agree on eleven. I'll ring Jack's mum and ask her and then we'll see.

2

Customer: I'd like to buy this handbag. But it's a bit dirty.

Shop assistant: We have another one like it here in light blue. Is this one okay?

Customer: I prefer the dark blue one really and I think there's only one.

Shop assistant: Yes, that's right. Would you like me to see if I can clean it for you?

Customer: Cleaning might make it worse. I would really prefer a discount. I like this bag.

Shop assistant: Well, I can offer you a discount of 5%. That's €10.
Customer: That would be okay. Thank you.

3
Customer: I'd also like to know how much Internet access will cost.
Mobile phone provider: It's €29.95 for unlimited phone calls and Internet access up to 20 gigabytes.
Customer: I've heard from a friend that he has the same for €20. Can you offer me a similar price?
Mobile phone provider: We can go down a bit with the price. What about €25?
Customer: Well, I don't really want to change providers and have a new number so I'll accept that price.

4
Tom: Darling, why don't we go to the cinema tonight? The new film about Tony Blair is on. I'd like to see it.
Jill: I don't think I really want to go to the cinema. I'm too hungry. I think I'd rather try the new Italian restaurant that has just opened.
Tom: I can cook something before we go and we could have a drink at the Italian place afterwards. And we could also eat something if you are still hungry after the film.
Jill: That sounds much better. I think I can agree to that.

Unit 11 – Extra practice

29

2b
See track 27.

Unit 12 What next?

30

2a
Naomi: I'm not really a good person to ask about technology because I'm not really interested in it, I just use it. I prefer knitting, sewing and cooking! Let me think … well, the first bit of technology I can remember actually using was a cassette player called *My First Sony*. I was about five. I actually think the cassette player belonged to my older brother Gabriel who was nine but he got something else so I could use it to listen to my cassettes and I had to keep it away from my little sister who was only two! My dad worked with computers so we always had them at home and there was one for all of us children to use in the basement. I got my first notebook for my eighteenth birthday. I was really more interested in TV before that and bought my first TV when I was fifteen with money I saved. My parents were not all that keen on me having my own TV. I watched lots of hospital soaps and now that I am a doctor they can see that maybe it was useful! I think I got my first mobile when I was about sixteen, which is pretty late for kids nowadays. I got a smartphone about two years ago. I can't imagine what will come next but I would quite like to have an iPad. My Mum has just got one and thinks it's great.

31

3a
Gary: ... Don't you think people will think more about healthy eating? So, we'll probably eat less meat and more organically grown fruit and vegetables?
Helen: I don't know really, there are so many scandals happening that I don't believe a lot of what it says in adverts. I think people will go for the cheapest food and hope for the best.
Gary: Well, I definitely eat less prepared food and make more myself so I know what is in what I eat – no old meat or horsemeat for instance.
Helen: I think maybe no meat at all is the best way but I just love a steak now and again. I even know vegetarians who say that!
Tony: I know I eat much more exotic food than my parents did. We go to Korean, Thai, Indian and African restaurants and often know all about the food even though we've never been to the countries.
Helen: But travel is also becoming so much cheaper and easier. People travel all over the world nowadays. That's a real advantage to globalization.
Tony: Yeah, but I think sometimes tourists forget that cultures are still different and behave in ways which upset people or are even dangerous. There are still a lot of poor people in the world even if tourism brings money into their countries. Tourism has meant more crime in some countries. And I heard that Internet crime often starts in poorer countries. People can earn money, for instance,

by writing these emails promising money, you know, these email scams. And tourists are often an easy target for robbers and muggers.

Gary: That's a reason for me not to travel to some countries. I really don't want to seem like a king in a five-star hotel when there are people who are hungry next door.

Tony: It's actually better to work or study in another country anyway than to go as a tourist. Students often spend a term or do an internship abroad so they can get to know the country.

Helen: That is a really good thing about education nowadays, learning about other countries and customs. It is a pity communication is always in English though!

Gary: What do you mean – a pity? Life is much easier if we all speak the same language!

Helen: I don't agree at all ...

Unit 12 - Extra practice

32

2a

See track 30.

33

2b

See track 31.

Key

Unit 1

2a (1) Hungarian, (2) Indian, (3) German

2b *Monika*: (certainly) Hungarian, German and English; *Madhu*: Hindi, English, Spanish and (certainly) German; *Sebastian*: German, English

2c (1) Madhu, (2) Monika, (3) Sebastian

2d (1) was, went; (2) became, needed; (3) had; (4) moved, have been living; (5) am, feel

3e 1d, 2a, 3e, 4b, 5c

Unit 1 – Extra Practice

1 (1) Where was Eva born? (2) How many brothers and sisters has she got? (3) What kind of pets did she have? (4) Where did she go to school? (5) What was her job?

2 3a, 4b, 1c, 2d, 5e

3a (1) Have you got any children? (2) Where do you live now? (3) Do you still work as a kindergarten teacher? (4) What is / was the strangest thing that happened to you?

4b (1) have got, (2) live, (3) work, (4) fell

5 *(possible answers)*
personal information: favourite film, driving licence, adventurous, holiday, family, play the guitar, travel, favourite place, reliable
job / professional life: engineer, actor, application form, customers, making phone calls, agency, employees, au pair, office
learning English: course, school, brush up my English

Unit 2

1b *(possible answers)*
Personal information: name, gender, date of birth, position, email address, status, telephone number, hometown
Interests: music, reading, cooking, languages, film, sports

3b (1) acquaintance; (2) partner; (3) buddy, chum, pal; (4) classmate; (5) companion

3d *Speaker 1*: People like to know what their friends are doing. *Speaker 2*: People only join Facebook because their friends do. *Speaker 3*: Facebook is a great business idea. *Speaker 4*: Facebook is not for everybody.

4a *age*: 41, *nationality*: Israeli, *family*: father, *job*: graphic designer

4b *(possible answers)*
(1) He told the Iranian people on his Facebook page that he loved them. He designed his message in a happy, innocent way with nice colours and hearts.
(2) On the same day, about 40,000 Israelis put their families' happy smiles on the Internet. More than 56 million people clicked the site. People wrote songs about their sympathy for the Iranians. Iranians put a peace message with music for the Israelis on the Internet. Two new pages appeared: Israellovesiran.com and Iranlovesisrael.com.

Unit 2 – Extra Practice

1 family, grandmother, niece; status, married, divorced; position, manager, waitress; nationality, English, French; likes, reading, cooking; feelings, excited, worried

2a (1) can find out, (2) like feeling, (3) interesting because, (4) for people under about … in my opinion

2b Lisa is quite happy with her life in Katherine. She works in the local supermarket and meets a lot of tourists who are on their way to Kakadu National Park. However, she's divorced now, she's forty-four, the kids are out of the house and live their own lives, and despite the fact that she likes going to the Diggers Tavern for a beer with her friend, Janine, she sometimes feels it's a bit boring in her small town, and it would be nice to have a few more friends. She enjoys having a good conversation, barbecues and picnics, playing tennis in the cool evening hours, and walking with her dog, T-Bone. She is toying with the idea of joining Facebook.

2c 1c, 2d, 3b, 4a

3 (1) What did you do in Alice Springs? (2) What's the story about this regatta? (3) Did everybody know each other through Facebook? (4) What did you talk about?

Unit 3

2a Denmark

2b 1d, 2e, 3a, 4c, 5b

4a 1

4d Eri: Japan; Juan: Mexico; Sabrina: London

4e *(possible answers)*
What made them happy when they were children?
Eri: watching Japanese TV; Juan: his birthdays; Sabrina: playing with other kids.
What's their tip for being happy?
Eri: enjoy every single day; Juan: meet friends and family as often as you can; Sabrina: do voluntary work

Unit 3 – Extra Practice

1 *(possible answers)*
scenery, beaches, probably, health, landscape, padlock, sweetheart, slightly / sweethearts, lightly

2 (1) A *hamster* is an animal, all the others are plants.
(2) *Italy* is a country, all the others are nationalities.
(3) *enjoy* is a verb, all the others are adjectives.
(4) *lake* is a noun, all the others are verbs.
(5) *see* is a verb, all the others are nouns which have to do with nature.
(6) *watching TV* is an indoor activity, all the others are outdoor activities.

3 (1) greatest; (2) as much ice cream as; (3) as often as you, happier

4 (1) happy, happier, happiest; (2) good, better, best; (3) beautiful, more beautiful, most beautiful; (4) big, bigger, biggest; (5) expensive, more expensive, most expensive

5 (1) more expensive than; (2) higher than; (3) as impressive as / more impressive than; (4) happiest; (5) as beautiful as / more beautiful than; (6) cheaper than

8 Dear Maria,
How are you? I hope you're fine and looking forward to Christmas! I visited a business partner in Denmark last week, and he invited me for dinner. Now guess where? A Mexican restaurant! It was really funny to see what the Danish think is Mexican food. The tortilla was sweeter than our Christmas cake, and the chilli con carne didn't have a single chilli! But the wine was as delicious as our wine at home – thank goodness!
See you soon
Love,
Juan

Unit 4

1c (1) go, (2) buy, (3) spend, (4) earn, (5) borrow, (6) lend

4a 1c, 2a, 3b

4b 3

4c *(possible answers)*
(1) Lonemoney has 673 offices. (2) You can borrow $24,000. (3) You have to pay it back in six months. (4) You can borrow up to seventy per cent of the value of the wine.

5c (1) He goes to skips in the evening and gets the food which shops throw away. (2) He grows his own fruit and vegetables. (3) Friends gave him one. (4) On foot or by bike.

Unit 4 – Extra Practice

1a expensive, security, branch, value, price, loan, bank

1b (1) Money can't buy you love.
(2) Don't spend your money before you earn it.
(3) Don't borrow or lend for a happy end.

1c cheap, cost, sell, pay

1d to lend, to spend

2a 1e, 2a, 3c, 4b, 5d

2b 42.195 km

3 (1) spending; (2) borrow, lend; (3) cost;
(4) spend, earn; (5) pay

4 (1) There is always more than we need.
(2) Helly can eat noodles every day.
(3) A fridge usually costs money.
(4) We never spend any money.
(5) We often drink milk.

5 *much*: coffee, shampoo, money, wine
many: friends, eggs, fridges, flats, offices, clothes

Unit 5

1c doing a sickie (1), fare-dodging (2), stealing (4), cheating (6), jaywalking (3), piracy (5)

1e *(possible answers)*
(1) There are many reasons why pupils cheat and are dishonest: pressure from the parents, heavy workload, too many tests on one day, etc. (2) If pupils have cheat sheets or notes, they will fail the test.

2b (1) had, (2) drove, (3) took, (4) drank,
(5) thought, (6) caught, (7) said

4a 1c, 2d, 3a, 4b, 5f, 6e, 7h, 8g

4c (1) a killer, (2) vandal, (3) kidnapper,
(4) hijacker, (5) robber

4d *(possible answers)*
A *shoplifter* is someone who steals something from a shop.
A *mugger* is someone who attacks people in public places and steals their money.
A *burglar* is someone who enters a building illegally in order to steal things.

4e *(possible answers)*
prison: an institution where people are kept for committing a crime
fine: an amount of money you have to pay because you have broken the law
probation: a system by which someone who has committed a crime is not sent to prison, but has to agree not to break the law again and let a probation officer check their behaviour for a specific period of time
community service: work that somebody does as a punishment, instead of going to prison

5d *(possible answers)*
Britain: 70 mph (about 113 kph); Abu Dhabi: 87 mph (140 kph); Czech Republic: 81 mph (130 kph); Romania: 81 mph (130 kph); Denmark: 81 mph (130 kph); Sweden: 69 mph (110 kph); Latvia: 69 mph (110 kph); Moldova: 69 mph (110 kph); Belgium: 74 mph (120 kph); Spain: 74 mph (120 kph); Switzerland: 74 mph (120 kph); Utah: 80 mph (129 kph); Hawaii: 60 mph (97 kph)

Unit 5 – Extra Practice

1 copy in a class test, travelling without a ticket, taking printer paper home from work, cheat in a test, do a sickie, play the piano at midday, wash your car on Sunday, steal from a shop

2 give, gave, given; spend, spent, spent;
see, saw, seen; feel, felt, felt;
be, was / were, been; have, had, had;
do, did, done

3a *(possible answers)*
(1) No, never.
(2) Six years.
(3) It's Sequoia National Park in Sierra Nevada, California.

3b (1) gave, (2) have seen, (3) have felt, (4) was born, (5) was, (6) started, (7) had, (8) saw, (9) have done, (10) have never had, (11) have not visited

4 (1) Have you ever worked
(2) Have you ever read
(3) Have you ever been
(4) Have you ever felt
(5) Have you ever travelled
(6) Have you ever seen
(7) Have you ever been

Unit 6

1b *(possible answer)*
She's annoyed because the garlic she bought is from Argentina.

1c 1c, 2a, 3e, 4b, 5d

2b *(possible answers)*
She is furious because …
… garlic is imported from Argentina.
… garlic could be bought / sold locally.
… of the transport costs.
… of the air pollution.
… she feels stupid / cheated.

3b 1e, 2f, 3b, 4d, 5a, 6c

3c *(possible answers)*
(1) *Freshly Farmed* delivers high quality food / organic produce.
(2) They deliver directly to your home or office, weekly, every other week, or monthly. You can cancel any time and you can customize your delivery.

4b (1) Vertical gardening, (2) Vertical farming

4d 1b, 2a

Unit 6 – Extra Practice

1 *(possible answers)*
places: garden, farm, supermarket, shop
adjectives: local, furious, healthy, organic, fresh, mouth-watering
what I like: pineapple, pear, kiwi, orange
people: teenager, young father
transport: car, bike
verbs: grow, believe, fly, buy, think, deliver

4 (1) lately, (2) as usual, (3) vegetables, (4) buy, (5) much, (6) home, (7) read

5 (1) I used to play volleyball, but now I play computer games.
(2) I used to spend my holiday in Italy, but now I fly to exotic countries.
(3) I used to go skiing, but now I go hiking.
(4) I used to smoke, but now I eat a lot of cake.
(5) I used to wear miniskirts, but now I wear trousers.
(6) I used to buy records, but now I download music from the Internet.
(7) I used to be poor, but now I'm rich.
(8) I used to buy things in shops, but now I buy online.

6 *(possible answers)*
(1) More and more people are buying organic food in the supermarket.
(2) More and more people are using their bicycles to go to work.
(3) More and more people are using social networks to stay in touch.
(4) More and more people are buying electric cars.
(5) More and more families are having a picnic on Sunday afternoons.

Unit 7

1b an egg

2a 1f, 2d, 3b, 4a, 5c, 6e

2c (1) rainforest, (2) tribes, (3) territory, (4) hunting, (5) bows and arrows, (6) crops

3a (1) Have you ever met a person from an "exotic" country?
(2) Have you ever heard a very unusual language?
(3) Have you ever travelled on a big river?
(4) Have you ever spoken to a fisherman?
(5) Have you ever been to the rainforest?
(6) Have you ever visited South America?
(7) Have you ever met a hunter?

3b *(possible answers)*
(1) Which country was it? (2) Which language was it? (3) Where did you go? (4) What did he say? (5) What was it like? (6) When did you go? (7) What did he say?

4a cooker, solar, lamp, energy, electrical, power, benefit

4c *(possible answers)*
(1) People who bring some sort of change into the world. (2) Brazil. (3) About one million people.

4d (1) some sort of change (2) You mean (3) What exactly (4) This means (5) what you are saying is (6) I didn't really get that. What are they?

4f A machine used to generate electricity.

4g fuel, these, normally, islands, need, buy, convenient, produce

Unit 7 – Extra Practice

1 *Across*: (3) tribe, (6) fisherman, (10) fuel, (11) island, (12) electricity
Down: (1) freezer, (2) hospital, (4) river, (5) paddle, (7) hunt, (8) benefit, (9) jungle

2a (1) massive change, (2) benefits of energy, (3) supply of electrical power, (4) far away from civilization, (5) more than one million people

2b (1) a generator powered by fuel, (2) access to electrical power, (3) just in case of a power shortage, (4) they paddle their canoes, (5) they produce energy without any trouble

3 Australia

4 (1) How often have you been to Australia? When were you there last?
(2) Have you ever seen kangaroos? How fast can they run?
(3) They say koalas make noises like bulls. Have you ever heard them?
(4) Have you ever travelled through the outback? What did you take for the trip?
(5) I know you like operas. Have you ever been to Sydney Opera House?
(6) Have you ever tried playing the didgeridoo? Can I learn to play it?

5 (1) hardly, (2) to, (3) was, (4) as, (5) would, (6) dangerous, (7) lose, (8) some, (9) safe, (10) want to

6a *(possible answers)*
(1) Have you ever lost your passport? Where was it?
(2) Have you ever lost your way in a foreign country? How did you manage to find your way back?
(3) Have you ever spent a holiday on a boat? When was it?
(4) Have you ever spent a night at an airport? Did you sleep well?
(5) Have you ever travelled in a hot air balloon? Were you scared?
(6) Have you ever been to a horrible hotel? Where was it?

Unit 8

1a a hotel resort without TV, mobile phones and Internet access

1b (4) Slow thinking is deep thinking
(2) An expensive privilege
(5) So what can we do?

1e 1b, 2a, 3c, 4b, 5a

2a 1a, 2c, 3e, 4b, 5f, 6d

2b *(possible answers)*
(1) used, (2) sent / written, (3) sent, (4) sent / written, (5) made, (6) written / sent

2d 5a, 3b, 1c, 4d, 2e, 6f

3c (1) make me, (2) let me

Unit 8 – Extra Practice

1 (1) message, (2) yoga, (3) mobile, (4) magazine, (5) resort, (6) pigeon, (7) peaceful, (8) rural, (9) airmail, (10) selfish

2a text

2b 1

3 (1) let, (2) let, (3) lets, (4) makes, (5) make, (6) let, (7) make, (8) made, (9) made, (10) let

4a 1

4b (1) were picked up, (2) taken, (3) were given, (4) was called, (5) 's / was made, (6) were shown

5 (1) Spanish Centre Playa del Carmen, Luisa speaking. How can I help you?
(2) Hello, this is Sandra speaking from Germany. I need some information on language learning courses.
(3) Wonderful! When would you like to come to Mexico?
(4) In our summer holidays, August or September.
(5) How long would you like to stay?
(6) Well, it depends on the price. I can't spend more than €1,800, and I would like to have lessons in the morning and excursions in the afternoon.
(7) OK, let me see … What level are you?
(8) I can understand a bit because I had Latin at school, but I can't speak it.

(9) So that would be a beginner's course. I can send you an offer for a three-week course with flight and accommodation with a host family here in Playa del Carmen. Can you give me your email address? I'll send you the information then.
(10) Of, course! My address is sandrahei@yahoo.com. Thanks for the information!
(11) You're welcome! Hasta luego.

Unit 9

2a guerrilla

2b (1) mayor, (2) derelict, (3) cosy, (4) bridge railing

2c (1) cosy, (2) mayor, (3) derelict, (4) bridge railing

2d *All answers are correct.*

2e (1) have your hair done, (2) have your windows cleaned, (3) have your tooth extracted (4) have your car serviced

3b true: She stopped collecting …
true: She doesn't keep …

Unit 9 – Extra Practice

2 *(possible answers)*
How long have you had this old-fashioned pair of glasses, dear?
How long have you had / worn this worn-out pullover?
How long have you had / carried / used this old handbag?
How long have you had / used / worn this awful watch?
How long have you had / worn this old coat?

3a (1) really think (2) you agree (3) sick and tired (4) Actually (5) other hand

4a Dorothy is having her hair cut.

4b *Dorothy:* (1) my picture taken (2) have a spare key made (3) have it cleaned
Betty: (1) to have it fixed (2) have it serviced (3) have my hair cut

5 (1) won, (2) had, (3) had, (4) had, (5) travelled, (6) visited

Unit 10

1b *from left to right:* (2) (Juliet), (1) (Charlotte), (4) (David), (3) (Sam)

1c (1) Charlotte, (2) David, (3) Juliet, (4) Juliet, (5) Charlotte, (6) David

2a 1h, 2f, 3d, 4a, 5g, 6e, 7c, 8b

2b (1) restaurant critic, (2) personal shopper, (3) waiter, (4) journalist, (5) pilot, (6) chambermaid, (7) call centre operator, (8) photographer

3b (1) India, (2) Wales, (3) Canada, (4) South Africa, (5) Ghana, (6) China, (7) Sweden

3d (1) difficult / accent, (2) easy / vocabulary, (3) easy / grammar

4a 1e, 2a, 3f, 4g, 5c, 6d, 7b

Unit 10 – Extra Practice

1 (1) customer, (2) pilot, (3) pension, (4) job, (5) Welsh

2 (1) false, (2) true, (3) true, (4) true, (5) false

3a (1) retire, (2) earn, (3) colleagues, (4) home office, (5) freelance, (6) standard of living, (7) freedom, (8) inherited, (9) live on the rent, (10) meaningful, (11) enough work

3b (1) I wish I could retire soon. (2) If I had more time I would like to do many other things. (3) If I had more money I would not be happier. (4) I wouldn't want to change my life. (5) If I didn't have any houses I would have to work. (6) If I didn't draw pictures for children's books my life would be less meaningful.

5 1b: security guard; 2f: additional job; 3d: know-it-all; 4c: small window in the door, used to check who the visitor is; 5a: a boat you cannot see because it moves under water; 6e: German Oktoberfest music

Unit 11

1d *(possible answers)*
money: golden handshake, pension
workplaces: company, house, factory
activities: advising, write, share, look after, work, clean, go shopping, cook, play cards

2a (3) replying to a job application, (2) spending free time together, (1) refusing an invitation, (4) asking a favour

2b formal: Dear …, Best wishes, With best wishes, All the best
informal: Hi, … see you later

3a *(possible answers)*
Ralph: I'm a pilot so my job is travelling so I couldn't do it if I didn't like travelling.
Marianne: I don't like flying and would hate to travel for my work.
Dieter: I'm not really a chauffeur but as I really enjoy driving, I think it might be a good job to have. I see different parts of the country and that's fine for me.
Vicki: I'm not sure if I want to travel more …

4b *(possible answers)*
(1) midnight / ten / eleven
(2) the fact that the handbag is a bit dirty / another handbag (in light blue) / a discount of 5%
(3) a price which is similar to the one his friend pays / go down to €25 / €25
(4) to go to the cinema / to go to the new Italian restaurant / him cooking something before they go to the cinema and on having a drink at the Italian place after the cinema

4c 1d, 2c, 3h, 4g, 5f, 6e, 7b, 8a

Unit 11 – Extra Practice

1a 1h, 2c, 3d, 4j, 5b, 6f, 7e, 8g, 9a, 10i

2a *Across:* (2) holiday, (5) company, (6) chauffeur, (7) tourist, (9) meetings, (12) presents, (13) passenger
Down: (1) pilot, (3) disadvantage, (4) strange, (8) village, (10) scared, (11) visit

2b (1) pilot, (2) tourist, (3) disadvantage, (4) holiday, (5) passenger, (6) visit, (7) scared, (8) village, (9) company, (10) meetings, (11) chauffeur, (12) travelling, (13) strange, (14) presents
(*travelling* is not in the crossword)

Unit 12

1a *top photos:* 3, 2
bottom photos: 1, 4

1c *(possible answers)*
(1) You only need a mobile phone.
(2) They come from the sounds birds make.
(3) They use them to make money.
(4) You can plant flowers, vegetables or fruit in them.
(5) Because they don't have to travel to work.

2a *from top to bottom:* cassette player, first TV, first mobile, first notebook, smartphone, iPad

2b family

3a Food, Travel, Education

3b *(possible answers)*
Food, positive: we'll probably eat less meat and more organically grown fruit and vegetables
Food, negative: people will go for the cheapest food
travel, positive: cheaper and easier
travel, negative: tourists forget that cultures are still different and behave in ways which upset people or are even dangerous
education, positive: learning about other countries and customs
education, negative: communication is always in English

3d 1f, 2c, 3e, 4b, 5d, 6a

Unit 12 – Extra Practice

1a Twitter, email, engaged, device, organic, old-timer, savings, eventually, environment, technology

1b sack garden, cassette player, home office, developing countries, organic food, email scam, well-known, self-employed, hospital soaps

2a technology, cassette player, hospital soaps

2b (1) fruit, (2) food, (3) horsemeat, (4) vegetarians, (5) know, (6) also, (7) people, (8) money, (9) by, (10) than, (11) though

2c *(possible answers)*
Growing organic food will become big business.
Speaking more than one language will be more important.
People will eat less prepared food.

3 *(possible answers)*
Extra Practice Unit 1: What does Eva do in the long winters at the North Cape? *Answer:* She knits pullovers for the tourists who want a souvenir from the North Cape.
Extra Practice Unit 2: Where did Lisa and Janine go in order to meet their new friends from Facebook? *Answer*: They travelled to Alice Springs to the Todd River Regatta.
Extra Practice Unit 3: Where did Juan's business partner invite him for dinner? *Answer*: To a Mexican restaurant in Denmark.
Extra Practice Unit 4: What can Helly eat every day? *Answer*: She can eat noodles every day.
Extra Practice Unit 5: How much money did Susanne have for her first trip to Italy? *Answer*: She had 400 German marks (€ 200) for four weeks.
Extra Practice Unit 6: Which trend does the picture in exercise 6.2 show? *Answer*: More and more people are going by bike.
Extra Practice Unit 7: What is the name of the traditional instrument played by the Aborigines in Australia? *Answer*: It's the didgeridoo.
Extra Practice Unit 8: What was Anna's non-alcoholic drink called? *Answer*: Tropical Magic.
Extra Practice Unit 9: What would Betty and Dorothy do if they won £ 10,000 at the bingo hall? *Answer*: They would buy a lot of wool.
Extra Practice Unit 10: What does Sam live on? *Answer*: Sam lives on the rent of the houses he inherited from his grandfather.
Extra Practice Unit 11: Why did Marianne fly only once in her life? *Answer*: She's afraid of flying but wanted to visit her daughter in America.
Extra Practice Unit 12: What did Naomi like to watch on TV when she was a teenager? *Answer*: She liked to watch hospital soaps.

Vocabulary unit by unit

The following list is in chronological order and contains language (words and phrases) we have chosen for Level B1. We assume you will be familiar with the language for Levels A1 and A2. The meaning used in the unit is the one given here, but there may also be other meanings for these words and phrases. We have not included words and phrases from the *Focus on reading* texts. We suggest that if you do not know what something means you use a good monolingual or bilingual dictionary.

T means the language is used in the recordings..

Module 1 You and me

Unit 1 A new start

1

personal ['pɜːsənl] persönlich
responsible [rɪ'spɒnsəbl] verantwortlich

2

Hungarian [hʌŋ'geəriən] Ungar(in)
Indian ['ɪndiən] Inder(in)
brush up T [ˌbrʌʃ 'ʌp] auffrischen
application form T [ˌæplɪ'keɪʃn ˌfɔːm] Bewerbungsformular
feeling T ['fiːlɪŋ] Gefühl
shy T [ʃaɪ] schüchtern
Hungary T ['hʌŋgəri] Ungarn
lyrics T ['lɪrɪks] Liedtext
Hindi T ['hɪndi] Hindi-Amtssprache in Indien
look forward to T [ˌlʊk 'fɔːwəd tʊ] sich freuen auf
not my cup of tea T [ˌnɒt 'maɪ kʌp‿əv ˌtiː] nicht meine Sache
deal with T ['diːl wɪð] zurecht kommen mit
fluent ['fluːənt] fließend

3

abroad [ə'brɔːd] im Ausland
registered ['redʒɪstəd] angemeldet
host family ['həʊst ˌfæmli] Gastfamilie
independence [ˌɪndɪ'pendəns] Unabhängigkeit
in demand [ɪn dɪ'mɑːnd] (nach)gefragt
reliable [rɪ'laɪəbl] zuverlässig
inquiry [ɪn'kwaɪəri] Anfrage
employee [ɪm'plɔɪiː] Angestellte(r)
apply for a position [əˌplaɪ fər‿ə pə'zɪʃn] sich auf eine Stelle bewerben
pick up somebody [ˌpɪk 'ʌp ˌsʌmbədi] jemanden abholen
the chemistry was good [ðə ˌkemɪstri wəz 'gʊd] die Chemie stimmte
room and board [ˌruːm ənd 'bɔːd] Unterkunft und Verpflegung
temporary grandma [ˌtemprəri 'grænmɑː] Großmutter auf Zeit
adventurous [əd'ventʃrəs] abenteuerlustig
retire [rɪ'taɪə] in den Ruhestand gehen

Unit 1 – Extra Practice

4

Santa Claus [ˌsæntə 'klɔːz] Weihnachtsmann
turn out to be [ˌtɜːn 'aʊt tə biː] sich herausstellen, dass
North Cape [ˌnɔːθ 'keɪp] Nordkap
Norway ['nɔːweɪ] Norwegen
knit [nɪt] stricken

Unit 2 Family & friends

1

gender ['dʒendə] Geschlecht
date of birth [ˌdeɪt‿əv 'bɜːθ] Geburtsdatum
female ['fiːmeɪl] weiblich
position [pə'zɪʃn] berufliche Position

interest ['ɪntrəst] Interesse
assistant head of marketing [əˌsɪstənt ˌhed‿əv 'mɑːkɪtɪŋ] stellvertretender Marketingleiter
status ['steɪtəs] Familienstand
retired [rɪ'taɪəd] im Ruhestand
freelance ['friːlɑːns] Freiberufler
personal information [ˌpɜːsnəl ˌɪnfə'meɪʃn] persönliche Angaben
divorced [dɪ'vɔːst] geschieden
be seeing someone [biː 'siːɪŋ ˌsʌmwʌn] mit jemandem zusammen sein

2

stepmother ['stepˌmʌðə] Stiefmutter
niece [niːs] Nichte
mother-in-law ['mʌðərɪnˌlɔː] Schwiegermutter
nephew ['nefjuː] Neffe
description [dɪ'skrɪpʃn] Beschreibung
large [lɑːdʒ] groß
patchwork ['pætʃwɜːk] Patchwork
valuable ['væljuəbl] wertvoll
marriage ['mærɪdʒ] Ehe
divorce [dɪ'vɔːs] Scheidung
get on well [get ˌɒn 'wel] gut auskommen
respect [rɪ'spekt] Respekt
celebrity [sə'lebrəti] Berühmtheit
stepson ['stepsʌn] Stiefsohn

3

acquaintance [ə'kweɪntəns] Bekannte(r)
buddy ['bʌdi] Kumpel
chum [tʃʌm] Kumpel
classmate ['klɑːsmeɪt] Klassenkamerad(in)
companion [kəm'pænjən] Gefährte (Gefährtin)
pal [pæl] Kumpel
informal [ɪn'fɔːml] informell
someone you are close to [ˌsʌmwʌn ju ɑː 'kləʊs tʊ] jemand, dem du nahe bist
site T [saɪt] Website
hang out T [ˌhæŋ 'aʊt] rumhängen
sheep T [ʃiːp] Schaf
cattle T [kætl] Vieh
be connected to T [biː kə'nektɪd tʊ] verbunden sein mit
herd T [hɜːd] Herde
post something on Facebook T ['pəʊst ˌsʌmθɪŋ ɒn 'feɪsbʊk] etwas auf Facebook posten
even though T [ˌiːvn ðəʊ] obwohl
garbage T ['gɑːbɪdʒ] Müll
a complete waste of time and energy T [ə kəmˌpliːt 'weɪst‿əv ˌtaɪm ənd 'enədʒi] eine totale Verschwendung von Zeit und Mühe
be worth T [biː 'wɜːθ] wert sein
go public T [ˌgəʊ 'pʌblɪk] an die Börse gehen
advertiser T ['ædvətaɪzə] Werbekunde
get in touch T [ˌget ɪn 'tʌtʃ] in Verbindung treten
damage T ['dæmɪdʒ] zerstören
relationship T [rɪ'leɪʃnʃɪp] Beziehung
privacy settings T ['prɪvəsi ˌsetɪŋz] persönliche Sicherheitseinstellungen
virus T ['vaɪrəs] (Computer)virus
firmly believe [ˌfɜːmli bɪ'liːv] fest an etwas glauben
keep in touch [ˌkiːp ɪn 'tʌtʃ] in Kontakt bleiben

4

bomb [bɒm] Bombe
Israeli [ɪz'reɪli] Israeli
be fed up with something [biː ˌfed 'ʌp wɪð ˌsʌmθɪŋ] etwas satt haben
escalation [ˌeskə'leɪʃn] Eskalation
hatred ['heɪtrɪd] Hass
trigger ['trɪgə] auslösen
politician [ˌpɒlə'tɪʃn] Politiker
on both sides [ɒn 'bəʊθ ˌsaɪdz] auf beiden Seiten
make sense [ˌmeɪk 'sens] Sinn machen
Iranian [ɪ'reɪniən] Iraner(in)
graphic designer ['græfɪk dɪˌzaɪnə] Grafikdesigner(in)
innocent ['ɪnəsnt] unschuldig
in an innocent way [ɪn ən ˌɪnəsnt 'weɪ] auf unschuldige Art und Weise
appear [ə'pɪə] erscheinen
live and let live [ˌlɪv ən 'let lɪv] leben und leben lassen
show up [ˌʃəʊ 'ʌp] hingehen

Unit 2 – Extra practice

2

despite the fact [dɪˌspaɪt ðə ˈfækt] trotz der Tatsache
toy with an idea [ˌtɔɪ wɪð‿ən aɪˈdɪə] mit einer Idee spielen
Prince Charming [ˌprɪns ˈtʃɑːmɪŋ] Märchenprinz
chat [tʃæt] schwätzen
I see your point [aɪ ˈsiː jɔː ˌpɔɪnt] ich verstehe was du meinst
suppose [səˈpəʊz] annehmen
exception to the rule [ɪkˈsepʃn tə ðə ˌruːl] Ausnahme von der Regel
local [ˈləʊkl] Einheimische(r)
regatta [rɪˈgætə] Regatta
is held [ɪz ˈheld] wird durchgeführt
ironic [aɪˈrɒnɪk] ironisch
riverbed [ˈrɪvəbed] Flußbett
attract [əˈtrækt] anziehen
spectator [spekˈteɪtə] Zuschauer
bottomless [ˈbɒtəmles] ohne Boden
pick up [ˌpɪk ˈʌp] aufheben
competitor [kəmˈpetɪtə] Mitbewerber(in), Gegenspieler(in)
cancelled [ˈkænsld] abgesagt
due to [ˈdjuː tʊ] aufgrund
flooding [ˈflʌdɪŋ] Flut

Unit 3 Love and happiness

happiness [ˈhæpinəs] Glück

1

New Zealander [ˌnjuː ˈziːləndə] Neuseeländer
beautiful scenery [ˌbjuːtəfl ˈsiːnri] schöne Landschaft
disagree [ˌdɪsəˈgriː] anderer Meinung sein
strongly disagree [ˌstrɒŋli ˌdɪsəˈgriː] deutlich anderer Meinung sein
neither … nor [ˌnaɪðə … nɔː] weder … noch
slightly disagree [ˌslaɪtli ˌdɪsəˈgriː] ein wenig anderer Meinung sein
in most ways [ɪn ˈməʊst ˌweɪz] in vielerlei Hinsicht
ideal [aɪˈdɪəl] ideal
conditions of life [kənˌdɪʃnz əv ˈlaɪf] Lebensumstände
be satisfied with [biː ˈsætɪsfaɪd wɪð] zufrieden sein mit

2

followed by [ˈfɒləʊd baɪ] gefolgt von
Finland [ˈfɪnlənd] Finnland
the Netherlands [ðə ˈneðələndz] die Niederlande
expect to [ɪkˈspekt tʊ] erwarten
lead a happy life [ˌliːd‿ə ˌhæpi ˈlaɪf] ein glückliches Leben führen
in the near future [ɪn ðə ˌnɪə ˈfjuːtʃə] in naher Zukunft
take part [ˌteɪk ˈpɑːt] teilnehmen
study [ˈstʌdi] Studie
report [rɪˈpɔːt] berichten
sadness [ˈsædnɪs] Traurigkeit
enjoyment [ɪnˈdʒɔɪmənt] Vergnügen
take the top spot [ˌteɪk ðə ˌtɒp ˈspɒt] den ersten Rang einnehmen
Denmark [ˈdenmɑːk] Dänemark
fish dish [ˈfɪʃ dɪʃ] Fischgericht
Caribbean [ˌkærəˈbiːən] Karibik
school-leaver [ˈskuːl ˌliːvəz] Schulabgänger
go on [ˌgəʊ ˈɒn] fortsetzen
statistics [stəˈtɪstɪks] Statistik
excellent [ˈekslənt] ausgezeichnet
disadvantage [ˌdɪsədˈvɑːntɪdʒ] Nachteil
public transport [ˌpʌblɪk ˈtrænspɔːt] öffentlicher Verkehr
canoeing [kəˈnuːɪŋ] Kanufahren
the Danish [ðə ˈdeɪnɪʃ] die Dänen
social security [ˌsəʊʃl sɪˈkjʊərəti] soziale Sicherheit
wider variety of landscapes [ˈwaɪdə vəˌraɪəti əv ˈlændskeɪps] größere Vielfalt an Landschaft
so do I [ˌsəʊ du ˈaɪ] ich auch
neither do I [ˌnaɪðə du ˈaɪ] ich auch nicht
me neither [ˌmiː ˈnaɪðə] ich auch nicht

3

crocus [ˈkrəʊkəs] Krokus

4

love padlock [ˈlʌv ˌpædlɒk] Liebesschloss
lock [lɒk] Schloss
magic [ˈmædʒɪk] magisch
everlasting [ˌevəˈlɑːstɪŋ] immerwährend
curl [kɜːl] Locke
locked in [ˌlɒkt ˈɪn] eingeschlossen in

notice ['nəʊtɪs] wahrnehmen
wonder what they mean [ˌwʌndə wɒt ðeɪ 'miːn] sich fragen, was sie bedeuten
have a closer look [ˌhæv‿ə 'kləʊsə ˌlʊk] genauer hinsehen
shortly after ['ʃɔːtli ˌɑːftə] kurz nach
be published [biː 'pʌblɪʃt] veröffentlicht werden
swear [sweə] schwören
eternal [ɪ'tɜːnl] ewig
lamp post ['læmp pəʊst] Straßenlaterne
remove [rɪ'muːv] entfernen
in danger of collapsing [ɪn ˌdeɪndʒər‿əv kə'læpsɪŋ] in Gefahr sein, zusammenzubrechen
weight [weɪt] Gewicht

your turn T ['jɔː tɜːn] Sie sind an der Reihe
topic T ['tɒpɪk] Thema
Japanese T [ˌdʒæpə'niːz] Japaner(in)
career T [kə'rɪə] (berufliche) Karriere
financial security T [faɪˌnænʃl sɪ'kjʊərəti] finanzielle Sicherheit
be homesick T [biː 'həʊmsɪk] Heimweh haben
childhood T ['tʃaɪldhʊd] Kindheit
enormous T [ɪ'nɔːməs] riesig
I must admit T [aɪ ˌmʌst əd'mɪt] ich muss zugeben
voluntary work T [ˌvɒləntri 'wɜːk] ehrenamtliche Tätigkeit
local T ['ləʊkl] örtlich
Oxfam shop T ['ɒksfæm ˌʃɒp] Dritte-Welt-Laden

Module 2 The world around us

Unit 4 Money

1

lend [lend] jemandem etw. leihen
borrow ['bɒrəʊ] (sich) etw. von jemandem leihen

2

decimal point ['desɪml ˌpɔɪnt] Dezimalpunkt
full stop [ˌfʊl 'stɒp] Punkt (Satzzeichen)
it depends [ɪt dɪ'pendz] das hängt ganz davon ab

3

mattress ['mætrəs] Matratze
survey ['sɜːveɪ] Umfrage
savings ['seɪvɪŋz] Ersparnis
cake tin ['keɪk tɪn] Kuchenform
wardrobe ['wɔːdrəʊb] Kleiderschrank
take place [ˌteɪk 'pleɪs] stattfinden

4

loan [ləʊn] Darlehen
security [sɪ'kjʊərəti] Sicherheit
branch [brɑːnʃ] Zweigstelle
represent [ˌrepri'zent] vertreten
jewel ['dʒuːəl] Juwel
art [ɑːt] Kunst
in return for [ɪn rɪ'tɜːn fɔː] dafür
make a loan [ˌmeɪk‿ə 'ləʊn] ein Darlehen geben
about [ə'baʊt] ungefähr
value ['væljuː] Wert

5

grow [grəʊ] anbauen
feature T ['fiːtʃə] Programmpunkt
plenty of time T [ˌplenti‿əv 'taɪm] viel Zeit
skip T [skɪp] Müllcontainer
wasted T ['weɪstɪd] verschwendet
keen on doing something T [ˌkiːn ɒn 'duːɪŋ ˌsʌmθɪŋ] etwas sehr gerne tun
gardening T ['gɑːdnɪŋ] Gartenarbeit
freeze T [friːz] einfrieren
freezer T ['friːzə] Gefriergerät
time is running out T ['taɪm ɪz ˌrʌnɪŋ 'aʊt] wir haben keine Zeit mehr

6

be in good condition [biː ɪn ˌgʊd kən'dɪʃn] in einem guten Zustand sein

Unit 5 Crime and punishment

crime [kraɪm] Kriminalität
punishment ['pʌnɪsmənt] Strafe

1

phone in sick [ˌfəʊn ɪn ˈsɪk] sich telefonisch krank melden

printer paper [ˈprɪntə ˌpeɪpə] Druckerpapier

copy [ˈkɒpi] abschreiben

do a sickie [ˌduː‿ ə ˈsɪki] „krank machen"

fare-dodging [ˈfeəˌdɒdʒɪŋ] schwarzfahren

cheat [tʃiːt] täuschen, mogeln, spicken

jay-walking [ˈdʒeɪˌwɔːkɪŋ] regelwidriges Überqueren einer Straße

piracy [ˈpaɪrəsi] Piraterie

dishonest T [dɪsˈɒnɪst] unehrlich

pressure T [ˈpreʃə] Druck

heavy workload T [ˌhevi ˈwɜːkləʊd] hohe Arbeitsbelastung

make sure that T [ˌmeɪk ˈʃɔː ˈðæt] darauf achten, dass

encourage T [ɪnˈkʌrɪdʒ] ermuntern

be punished T [biː ˈpʌnɪʃt] bestraft werden

cheat sheet T [ˈtʃiːt ʃiːt] Spickzettel

fail the test T [ˌfeɪl ðə ˈtest] bei der Prüfung durchfallen

2

shopping trolley [ˈʃɒpɪŋ ˌtrɒli] Einkaufswagen

at midday [ət ˌmɪdˈdeɪ] um die Mittagszeit

fine [faɪn] Geldstrafe

ride [raɪd] Fahrt

unfortunately [ʌnˈfɔːtʃnətli] leider

judge [dʒʌdʒ] Richter

3

mow the lawn [ˌməʊ ðə ˈlɔːn] den Rasen mähen

complain [kəmˈpleɪn] sich beschweren

advice [ədˈvaɪs] Rat

4

hijacking [ˈhaɪdʒækɪŋ] Entführung

robbery [ˈrɒbəri] Raub

vandalism [ˈvændəlɪzm] Vandalismus

pickpocketing [ˈpɪkˌpɒkɪtɪŋ] Taschendiebstahl

burglary [ˈbɜːgləri] Einbruch

mugging [ˈmʌgɪŋ] Straßenraub

shoplifting [ˈʃɒpˌlɪftɪŋ] Ladendiebstahl

difference [ˈdɪfrəns] Unterschied

damage [ˈdæmɪdʒ] beschädigen

property [ˈprɒpəti] Eigentum

by force [baɪ ˈfɔːs] mit Gewalt

shoplifter [ˈʃɒpˌlɪftə] Ladendieb

mugger [ˈmʌgə] Straßenräuber

burglar [ˈbɜːglə] Einbrecher

probation [prəˈbeɪʃn] Bewährung

do community service [du kəˈmjuːnəti ˌsɜːvɪs] gemeinnützige Arbeit leisten

5

wear seatbelts [ˌweə ˈsiːtbelts] Sicherheitsgurte tragen

speed limit [ˈspiːd ˌlɪmɪt] Geschwindigkeitsbegrenzung

mph, miles per hour [ˌempiːˈeɪtʃ, ˌmaɪlz pər‿ˈaʊə] Meilen pro Stunde

kph, kilometres per hour [ˌkeɪpiːˈeɪtʃ, kɪˌlɒmɪtəz pər‿ˈaʊə] Kilometer pro Stunde

on motorways [ɒn ˈməʊtəweɪz] auf Autobahnen

reduced [rɪˈdjuːst] herabgesetzt

recently [ˈriːsntli] kürzlich

average speed [ˌævrɪdʒ ˈspiːd] durchschnittliche Geschwindigkeit

island [ˈaɪlənd] Insel

off the west coast of England [ˌɒf ðə ˌwest ˈkəʊst əv ˈɪŋglənd] vor der Westküste Englands

motor racing [ˈməʊtə ˌreɪsɪŋ] Autorennen

in general [ɪn ˈdʒenrəl] im allgemeinen

fewer accidents [ˌfjuːər‿ˈæksɪdənts] weniger Unfälle

less fixed [ˌles ˈfɪkst] weniger starr

traffic conditions [ˈtræfɪk kənˌdɪʃnz] Verkehrsbedingungen

6

illegal [ɪˈliːgl] illegal

at a time [ˌæt ə ˈtaɪm] gleichzeitig

citizen [ˈsɪtɪzn] Bürger(in)

Unit 5 – Extra practice

3

chatter [ˈtʃætə] Geplapper

be amazed [biː əˈmeɪzd] erstaunt sein

remote [rɪˈməʊt] entlegen

be well off [biː ˌwel ˈɒf] reich sein

backpack ['bækpæk] mit dem Rucksack reisen
volcano [vɒl'keɪnəʊ] Vulkan
Christmas Eve [ˌkrɪsməs 'iːv] Heiligabend
giant ['dʒaɪənt] riesig

Unit 6 Does it matter?

does it matter? [ˌdʌz‿ɪt 'mætə] ist das wichtig?

1

pear [peə] Birne
means of transport [ˌmiːnz‿əv 'trænspɔːt] Transportmittel
strange T [streɪndʒ] seltsam
lately T ['leɪtli] kürzlich
as usual T [əz 'juːʒl] wie immer
especially T [ɪ'speʃli] besonders
courgette T [kɔː'ʒet] Zucchini
aubergine T ['əʊbəʒiːn] Aubergine
garlic T ['gɑːlɪk] Knoblauch
the lot T [ðə 'lɒt] alles
convenient T [kən'viːniənt] bequem
stuff T [stʌf] Zeug
just like that T [ˌdʒʌst laɪk 'ðæt] einfach so
glance at T ['glɑːns ət] einen Blick auf etw. werfen
label T ['leɪbl] Etikett
check [tʃek] prüfen
locally grown ['ləʊkli ˌgrəʊn] vor Ort angebaut
local farmer [ˌləʊkl 'fɑːmə] ein Bauer vor Ort

2

in heaven's name T [ɪn ˌhevnz 'neɪm] um Himmels willen
by the ton T [ˌbaɪ ðə 'tʌn] in rauhen Mengen
tasty T ['teɪsti] schmackhaft
including T [ɪn'kluːdɪŋ] einschließlich
fuel T ['fjuːəl] Brennstoff
freight ship T ['freɪt ʃɪp] Frachtschiff
air pollution T ['eə pəˌluːʃn] Luftverschmutzung
bulb of garlic T [ˌbʌlb‿əv 'gɑːlɪk] Knoblauchknolle
furious ['fjʊəriəs] wütend
far away places ['fɑːr‿əˌweɪ 'pleɪsɪz] weit entfernte Orte
compared to [kəm'peəd tʊ] verglichen mit
local product ['ləʊkl ˌprɒdʌkt] Produkt aus der Gegend

3

increasingly [ɪn'kriːsɪŋli] mehr und mehr
trusted ['trʌstɪd] vertrauenswürdig
join [dʒɔɪn] sich anschließen
nutrient rich ['njuːtriənt ˌrɪtʃ] nahrhaft
organic food [ɔːˌgænɪk 'fuːd] Bionahrung
customize ['kʌstəmaɪz] nach Kundenwünschen anfertigen
fertilizer ['fɜːtɪlaɪzə] Dünger
pesticide ['pestɪsaɪd] Pestizid
genetic manipulation [dʒɪˌnetɪk məˌnɪpjʊ'leɪʃn] Genmanipulation
member ['membə] Mitglied
adapt to your own needs [əˌdæpt tə jər‿'əʊn ˌniːdz] an eigene persönliche Bedürfnisse anpassen
full of healthy ingredients [ˌfʊl‿əv ˌhelθi ɪn'griːdiənts] mit vielen gesunden Zutaten
popular alternative [ˌpɒpjələ ɔːl'tɜːnətɪv] beliebte Alternative
regular ['regjələ] regelmässig
delivery [dɪ'lɪvri] Lieferung
mouth-watering ['maʊθ ˌwɔːtərɪŋ] appetitlich
organic produce [ɔːˌgænɪk 'prɒdjuːs] Bioprodukt
deliver [dɪ'lɪvə] liefern
cancel ['kænsl] abbestellen
commitment [kə'mɪtmənt] Verpflichtung
exclude something [ɪks'kluːd ˌsʌmθɪŋ] etwas ausschließen
item ['aɪtəm] Artikel
add [æd] hinzufügen
receive [rɪ'siːv] empfangen
satisfaction guaranteed [ˌsætɪs'fækʃn ˌgærən'tiːd] Zufriedenheit garantiert
delivery conditions [dɪ'lɪvri kənˌdɪʃnz] Lieferbedingungen

4

vertical ['vɜːtɪkl] vertikal
farming ['fɑːmɪŋ] Anbau
plant [plɑːnt] Pflanze
building ['bɪldɪŋ] Gebäude
live in harmony with [ˌlɪv ɪn 'hɑːməni wɪð] in Einklang leben mit

landscape designer ['lændskeɪp dɪˌzaɪnə]
Landschaftsarchitekt
all sorts of [ˌɔːl 'sɔːts‿əv] alle Arten von
indoors and outdoors [ˌɪndɔːz ənd 'aʊtdɔːz]
innen und außen
in any climate [ɪn 'eni ˌklaɪmət] in jedem Klima
this is a concept that argues [ˌðɪs‿ɪz ə ˌkɒnsept ðət 'ɑːgjuːz] dieses Konzept nimmt für sich in Anspruch
economical [ˌiːkə'nɒmɪkl] ökonomisch
environmental [ɪnˌvaɪrən'mentl] Umwelt-
viable ['vaɪəbl] machbar
cultivate ['kʌltɪveɪt] anbauen
plant or animal life [ˌplɑːnt ɔː 'ænɪml ˌlaɪf]
pflanzliches oder tierisches Leben

skyscraper ['skaɪˌskreɪpə] Wolkenkratzer
take the idea further [ˌteɪk ði aɪˌdɪə 'fɜːðə]
(gedanklich) weitergehen
legal permission [ˌliːgl pə'mɪʃn]
gesetzliche Genehmigung
brainwave ['breɪnweɪv] Geistesblitz
space [speɪs] Platz
grow vegetables locally [grəʊ ˌvedʒtəblz 'ləʊkəli]
Gemüse vor Ort anbauen
pumpkin ['pʌmpkɪn] Kürbis
rooster ['ruːstə] Hahn
crow [krəʊ] krähen
desperate ['desprət] verzweifelt

Module 3 Changes

Unit 7 Global Changes

1

define [dɪ'faɪn] definieren
it's kind of [ɪts ˌkaɪnd‿əv ...] es ist irgendwie

2

tribe [traɪb] Stamm
related [rɪ'leɪtid] verwandt
share [ʃeə] teilen
territory ['terətri] Gebiet
hunting ['hʌntɪŋ] Jagd
bows and arrows [ˌbəʊz ənd 'ærəʊz] Pfeil und Bogen
chase [tʃeɪs] jagen
rainforest ['reɪnˌfɒrɪst] Regenwald
tropical ['trɒpɪkl] tropisch
crops [krɒps] Feldfrüchte
divided [dɪ'vaɪdɪd] geteilt
plant-based ['plɑːntbeɪst] auf pflanzlicher Basis
poison ['pɔɪzn] Gift
shotgun ['ʃɒtgʌn] Schrotflinte
spear [spɪə] Speer
blowgun ['bləʊgʌn] Blasrohr
dart [dɑːt] Pfeil
tipped with poison [ˌtɪpt wɪð 'pɔɪzn]
die Spitze in Gift eingetaucht
nomadic [nəʊ'mædɪk] nomadisch
rely on [rɪ'laɪ ɒn] abhängig von
gather ['gæðə] sammeln

3

dialect ['daɪəlekt] Dialekt
unusual [ʌn'juːʒuəl] ungewöhnlich
hunter ['hʌntə] Jäger
jungle ['dʒʌŋgl] Dschungel
several times [ˌsevrəl 'taɪmz] mehrere Male

4

cooker ['kʊkə] Kocher
solar ['səʊlə] Solar
energy ['enədʒi] Energie
electrical power [ɪˌlektrɪkl 'paʊə] Strom
benefit ['benɪfɪt] Nutzen
broadcast T ['brɔːdkɑːst] Sendung
some sort of T ['sʌm ˌsɔːt‿əv] in irgendeiner Form
massive change T [ˌmæsɪv 'tʃeɪndʒ]
dramatischer Wandel
quite a few T [ˌkwaɪt‿ə 'fjuː] ziemlich viele
access T ['ækses] Zugang
regular supply T [ˌregjələ sə'plaɪ]
regelmäßige Versorgung
civilization T [ˌsɪvlaɪ'zeɪʃn] Zivilisation
genset T ['dʒenset] Generator

create T [kri'eɪt] erzeugen
I didn't really get that T [aɪ ˌdɪdnt ˌrɪəli 'get ðæt] das habe ich nicht wirklich verstanden
repeat [rɪ'piːt] wiederholen
fuel T ['fjuːəl] Brennstoff
electrical power from the grid T [ɪˌlektrɪkl 'paʊə frəm ðə 'grɪd] Strom aus dem Netz
far away T [ˌfɑːr‿ə'weɪ] weit entfernt
emergency T [ɪ'mɜːdʒənsi] Notfall
shortage T ['ʃɔːtɪdʒ] Knappheit
paddle T ['pædl] paddeln
canoe T [kə'nuː] Kanu
finally T ['faɪnli] schließlich
huge T [hjuːdʒ] riesig
convenient T [kən'viːniənt] bequem
definitively T [dɪ'fɪnətɪvli] sicher
solution T [sə'luːʃn] Lösung

5

switch off [ˌswɪtʃ 'ɒf] ausschalten
whenever [wen'evə] jedes Mal, wenn

Unit 7 – Extra practice

1

substance ['sʌbstəns] Substanz
surrounded by [sə'raʊndɪd baɪ] umgeben von
run [rʌn] betreiben

3

pouch [paʊtʃ] Beutel
huge [hjuːdʒ] riesig

5

cuddly ['kʌdli] knuddelig

6

hot-air balloon [ˌhɒt'eə bəˌluːn] Heißluftballon

Unit 8 (Dis)Connected?

connected [kə'nektɪd] verbunden
disconnected [ˌdɪskə'nektɪd] getrennt, abgeschnitten; hier: ohne Telefon- und Internetverbindung

1

cave [keɪv] Höhle
endangered [ɪn'deɪndʒəd] gefährdet
hotel resort [ˌhəʊtel rɪ'zɔːt] Hotelanlage
mobile phone [ˌməʊbaɪl 'fəʊn] Handy
Internet access ['ɪntənet ˌækses] Internetzugang
galaxy ['gæləksi] Galaxie
in space [ɪn 'speɪs] im Raum
be ahead of the crowd [biː ə'hed‿əv ðə ˌkraʊd] seiner Zeit voraus sein
world-famous [ˌwɜːld'feɪməs] weltberühmt
exaggerate [ɪg'zædʒəreɪt] übertreiben
unconventional [ˌʌnkən'venʃnəl] unkonventionell
unplugged [ʌn'plʌgd] unplugged („ausgesteckt", „ohne Strom")
growing number [ˌgrəʊɪŋ 'nʌmbə] wachsende Zahl
Internet connection ['ɪntənet kəˌnekʃn] Internet-Verbindung
precisely [prɪ'saɪsli] genau
constantly ['kɒnstəntli] ständig
average ['ævrɪdʒ] durchschnittlich
text message ['tekst ˌmesɪdʒ] SMS
rescue ['reskjuː] retten
insist on [ɪn'sɪst ɒn] bestehen auf
provide [prə'vaɪd] liefern
rural ['rʊərəl] ländlich
hustle and bustle [ˌhʌsl ənd 'bʌsl] Hektik
attention span [ə'tenʃn ˌspæn] Dauer der Konzentrationsfähigkeit
apparently [ə'pærəntli] offensichtlich
meaningful ['miːnɪŋfl] bedeutungsvoll
achieve [ə'tʃiːv] erreichen
loads of money [ˌləʊdz‿əv 'mʌni] Mengen von Geld
sanity ['sænəti] Gesundheit
selfish ['selfɪʃ] eigennützig
monk [mʌŋk] Mönch
nun [nʌn] Nonne
vital ['vaɪtl] sehr wichtig
reverse [rɪ'vɜːs] umkehren
inspiration [ˌɪnspə'reɪʃn] Inspiration
astronomy [ə'strɒnəmi] Astronomie
brain skills ['breɪn skɪlz] Fähigkeiten des Gehirns

2

carrier pigeon ['kæriə ˌpɪdʒən] Brieftaube

smoke signal ['sməʊk ˌsɪgnəl] Rauchzeichen

ancient ['eɪnʃnt] alt

3

advertisement T [əd'vɜːtɪsmənt] Anzeige

planet T ['plænɪt] Planet

block off T [ˌblɒk 'ɒf] blockieren

incoming and outgoing signals T [ˌɪnkʌmɪŋ ənd ˌaʊtkʌmɪŋ 'sɪgnəlz] ein- und abgehende Signale

you're kidding! T [ˌjɔː 'kɪdɪŋ] das ist doch nicht dein Ernst!

nightmare T ['naɪtmeə] Albtraum

when the sun sets T [ˌwen ðə 'sʌn ˌsets] wenn die Sonne untergeht

text T [tekst] eine SMS schreiben

deckchair T ['dektʃeə] Liegestuhl

diving ['daɪvɪŋ] T Tauchen

coral reef T [ˌkɒrəl 'riːf] Korallenriff

Unit 8 – Extra practice

1

gentle ['dʒentl] sanft

urban ['ɜːbən] städtisch

5

populous ['pɒpjələs] bevölkerungsreich

magnificent [mæg'nɪfɪsnt] großartig

enchanting [ɪn'tʃɑːntɪŋ] bezaubernd

excursion [ɪk'skɜːʃn] Ausflug

Unit 9 Unusual hobbies

2

back T [bæk] Rücken

ache T [eɪk] Schmerzen

I'm fine T [aɪm 'faɪn] mir geht's gut

guerrilla T [gə'rɪlə] Guerilla-

mayor T [meə] Bürgermeister

cosy T ['kəʊzi] Tee- / Eierwärmer

derelict T ['derəlɪkt] verlassen

depressing view T [dɪˌpresɪŋ 'vjuː] deprimierender Anblick

be sick and tired of something T [biː ˌsɪk ənd 'taɪəd əv ˌsʌmθɪŋ] etwas unerträglich finden

not quite T [ˌnɒt 'kwaɪt] nicht ganz

legal T ['liːgl] gesetzlich

bridge railing T [ˌbrɪdʒ 'reɪlɪŋ] Brückengeländer

in charge of [ɪn 'tʃɑːdʒ‿əv] verantwortlich für

run-down ['rʌndaʊn] runtergekommen

movement ['muːvmənt] Bewegung

be meant to [biː 'ment tʊ] sollen

term [tɜːm] Begriff

3

lovely ['lʌvli] hübsch

silver brooch [ˌsɪlvə 'brəʊtʃ] Silberbrosche

be shaped like [biː 'ʃeɪpt laɪk] geformt wie

bookend ['bʊkend] Buchstütze

table mat ['teɪbl mæt] Tischset

milk jug ['mɪlk dʒʌg] Milchkännchen

groundhopping ['graʊndˌhɒpɪŋ] Stadion-Hüpfen

involve [ɪn'vɒlv] beinhalten

attend [ə'tend] besuchen

stadium ['steɪdiəm] Stadion

originate [ə'rɪdʒəneɪt] den Ursprung haben

tie [taɪ] Krawatte

supporter [sə'pɔːtə] Fan

professional league [prə'feʃnəl ˌliːg] Fußball Bundes- und Regionalliga

geocaching ['dʒiːəʊˌkæʃɪŋ] Geocaching (eine Art Schnitzeljagd mit GPS)

participant [pɑː'tɪsɪpənt] Teilnehmer

GPS receiver [ˌdʒiːpiː'es rɪˌsiːvə] GPS Empfänger

hide and seek [ˌhaɪd‿n 'siːk] Versteck spielen

logbook ['lɒgbʊk] Logbuch

orienteering [ˌɔːriən'tɪərɪŋ] Orientierungslauf

treasure-hunting ['treʒəˌhʌntɪŋ] Schatzsuche

Cosplay ['kɒspleɪ] Cosplay

short for ['ʃɔːt fə] kurz für

performance art [pə'fɔːməns ˌɑːt] Kunstdarbietung

costume ['kɒstjuːm] Kostüm

accessory [ək'sesri] Accessoire

represent a character [ˌreprɪˌzent ə 'kærəktə] eine Figur darstellen

specific [spə'sɪfɪk] spezifisch

interact [ˌɪntə(r)'ækt] interagieren

create [kri'eɪt] herstellen
subculture ['sʌbˌkʌltʃə] Subkultur
be centered on [biː 'sentəd ɒn] bezogen auf
a broader use [ə 'brɔːdə ˌjuːs] Verwendung im weiteren Sinne
apply to [ə'plaɪ tʊ] gelten
venue ['venjuː] Veranstaltungsort
regardless of [rɪ'gɑːdləs əv] ungeachtet
cultural context [ˌkʌltʃrəl 'kɒntekst] kultureller Zusammenhang
source [sɔːs] Quelle
anime ['ɑːnimeɪ] japanische Zeichentrickfilme
enable [ɪ'neɪbl] befähigen
massive ['mæsɪv] enorm
growth [grəʊθ] Wachstum
pick up something as a hobby ['pɪk ʌp ˌsʌmθɪŋ æz‿ə 'hɒbi] etwas als Hobby wählen
phenomenon [fɪ'nɒmɪnən] Phänomen
popular culture [ˌpɒpjələ 'kʌltʃə] Popkultur
hidden treasures [ˌhɪdn 'treʒəz] versteckte Schätze

Unit 9 – Extra practice

4

railcard [reɪl kɑːd] Bahncard
spare key [ˌspeə 'kiː] Ersatzschlüssel
leak [liːk] undicht sein
have it fixed [ˌhæv‿ɪt 'fɪkst] etwas reparieren lassen
have it serviced [ˌhæv‿ɪt 'sɜːvɪst] in die Inspektion geben

Module 4 Work

Unit 10 Jobs and languages

1

enjoyable [ɪn'dʒɔɪəbl] angenehm
pleasant ['pleznt] nett
purpose ['pɜːpəs] Sinn
room maid T ['ruːm meɪd] Zimmermädchen
inherit T [ɪn'herɪt] erben
permanent job [ˌpɜːmənənt 'dʒɒb] Festanstellung
temporary job [ˌtemprəri 'dʒɒb] Zeitarbeit
be employed [biː ɪm'plɔɪd] eine Festanstellung haben

2

advise [əd'vaɪz] beraten
chambermaid ['tʃeɪmbəmeɪd] Zimmermädchen
tidy ['taɪdi] aufräumen
clumsy ['klʌmzi] ungeschickt

3

mother tongue [ˌmʌðə 'tʌŋ] Muttersprache
bilingual [baɪ'lɪŋgwəl] zweisprachig
cause confusion [ˌkɔːz kən'fjuːʒn] für Verwirrung sorgen
idiom ['ɪdiəm] Redewendung
saying ['seɪɪŋ] Redensart
proverb ['prɒvɜːb] Sprichwort
branch T [brɑːntʃ] Zweigstelle
interpreting [ɪn'tɜːprɪtɪŋ] Dolmetschen
negotiation [nɪˌgəʊʃi'eɪʃn] Verhandlung

Unit 11 Work and communication

1

break [breɪk] Pause
company outing [ˌkʌmpəni 'aʊtɪŋ] Betriebsausflug

2

job application ['dʒɒb æplɪˌkeɪʃn] Stellenbewerbung
require [rɪ'kwaɪə] benötigen
vacant ['veɪkənt] offen

3

long-haul flight T ['lɒŋhɔːl ˌflaɪt] Langstrecken-Flug
be scared T [biː 'skeəd] Angst haben
checkout assistant T ['tʃekaʊt əˌsɪstənt] Kassiererin
it suits me fine T [ɪt ˌsuːts mi 'faɪn] das passt mir
head of facilities T [ˌhed‿əv fə'sɪlətiz] Gebäudemanager

get fed up with something [ˌget fed ˈʌp wɪð ˌsʌmθɪŋ]
von etwas die Nase voll haben

satnav [ˈsætnæv] Navi

4

pay rise [ˈpeɪ raɪz] Gehaltserhöhung

similar T [ˈsɪmɪlə] ähnlich

Unit 11 – Extra practice

3

delay [dɪˈleɪ] Verzögerung

publisher [ˈpʌblɪʃə] Verleger

runny nose [ˌrʌni ˈnəʊz] laufende Nase

I'll keep you posted [aɪl ˌkiːp juː ˈpəʊstɪd]
ich halte dich auf dem Laufenden

Unit 12 What next?

1

device [dɪˈvaɪs] Gerät

nowadays [ˈnaʊədeɪz] heutzutage

pass on [ˌpɑːs ˈɒn] weiterleiten

character [ˈkærəktə] Zeichen

self-employed [ˌselfɪmˈplɔɪd] selbstständig

developing country [dɪˈveləpɪŋ ˌkʌntri]
Entwicklungsland

cloth [klɒθ] Stoff

2

sew T [səʊ] nähen

get engaged [ˌget ɪnˈgeɪdʒd] sich verloben

3

organically grown T [ɔːˌgænɪkli ˈgrəʊn]
biologisch angebaut

upset T [ʌpˈset] verärgern

internship T [ˈɪntɜːnʃɪp] Praktikum

bank cashier [ˌbæŋk kæˈʃɪə] jemand, der
am Schalter einer Bank arbeitet

cash machine [ˈkæʃ məˌʃiːn] Geldautomat

4

be caught speeding [biː ˌkɔːt ˈspiːdɪŋ] beim Überschreiten der Geschwindigkeit erwischt werden

retirement [rɪˈtaɪəmənt] Ruhestand

Alphabetical word list

The following list contains language (words and phrases) we have chosen for level B1. We assume you will be familiar with the language for Levels A1 and A2. The meaning used in the unit is the one given here, but there may also be other meanings for these words and phrases. We have not included words and phrases from the *Focus on reading* texts. We suggest that if you do not know what something means you use a good monolingual or bilingual dictionary.

The numbers after each entry show where a word comes up for the first time. *T* means the language is used on the CD and can be found in the Tapescripts, *EP* means the language is used in the Extra practice, for example:
6-3b Unit 6, exercise 3b
8-3c T Unit 8, exercise 3c, tapescripts
5-3a EP Unit 5, exercise 3a, extra practice

A

about ungefähr *4-4c*
abroad *im Ausland* *1-3a*
access Zugang *7-4c T*
accessory Accessoire *9-3d*
ache schmerzen *9-2a T*
achieve erreichen *8-1b*
acquaintance Bekannte(r) *2-3b*
adapt to anpassen an *6-3b*
add hinzufügen *6-3c*
admit zugeben *3-4d T*
adventurous abenteuerlustig *1-3d*
advertisement Anzeige *8-3c T*
advertiser Werbekunde *2-3d T*
advice Rat *5-3c*
advise beraten *10-2a*
(be) ahead of voraus (sein) *8-1b*
air pollution Luftverschmutzung *6-2a T*
(be) amazed erstaunt (sein) *5-3a EP*
ancient alt *8-2d*
anime japanische Zeichentrickfilme *9-3d*
apparently offensichtlich *8-1b*
appear erscheinen *2-4a*
application Bewerbung *11-2a*
application form Bewerbungsformular *1-2a T*
apply for sich bewerben *1-3d*
apply to gelten *9-3d*
argue sich für etwas aussprechen *6-4b*
art Kunst *4-4c*
arrow Pfeil *7-2a*
as usual wie immer *6-1b T*
assistant head of marketing stellvertretender Marketingleiter *2-1a*
astronomy Astronomie *8-1e*
attend besuchen *9-3d*
attention span Dauer der Konzentrationsfähigkeit *8-1b*
attract anziehen *2-2e EP*
aubergine Aubergine *6-1b T*
average durchschnittlich *8-1b*
average speed durchschnittliche Geschwindigkeit *5-5c*

B

back Rücken *9-2a T*
backpack mit dem Rucksack reisen *5-3a EP*
bank cashier jemand, der am Schalter einer Bank arbeitet *12-3c*
benefit Nutzen *7-4a*
bilingual zweisprachig *10-3b*
block off blockieren *8-3c T*
blowgun Blasrohr *7-2c*
board Verpflegung *1-3d*
bomb Bombe *2-4a*
bookend Buchstütze *9-3b*
borrow (sich) etw. von jemandem leihen *4-1c*
bottomless ohne Boden *2-2e EP*
bow Bogen *7-2a*
brain skills Fähigkeiten des Gehirns *8-1e*
brainwave Geistesblitz *6-4d*
branch Zweigstelle *4-4a*
break Pause *11-1b*
bridge railing Brückengeländer *9-2b T*

broadcast Sendung *7-4c T*
broader use Verwendung im weiteren Sinne *9-3d*
brooch Brosche *9-3b*
brush up auffrischen *1-2a T*
buddy Kumpel *2-3b*
building Gebäude *6-4b*
bulb of garlic Knoblauchknolle *6-2a T*
burglar Einbrecher *5-4d*
burglary Einbruch *5-4a*

C

cake tin Kuchenform *4-3b*
cancel abbestellen *6-3c*
cancelled abgesagt *2-2e EP*
canoe Kanu *7-4f T*
canoeing Kanufahren *3-2c*
career (berufliche) Karriere *3-4d T*
Caribbean Karibik *3-2b*
carrier pigeon Brieftaube *8-2a*
cash machine Geldautomat *12-3c*
cattle Vieh *2-3d T*
cause confusion für Verwirrung sorgen *10-3c*
cave Höhle *8-1a*
celebrity Berühmtheit *2-2c*
(be) centered on bezogen (sein) auf *9-3d*
chambermaid Zimmermädchen *10-2a*
character Figur, Zeichen *9-3d*
(in) charge of verantwortlich für *9-2c*
chase jagen *7-2a*
chat schwätzen *2-2c EP*
chatter Geplapper *5-3a EP*
cheat täuschen, mogeln, spicken *5-1c*
cheat sheet Spickzettel *5-1e T*
check prüfen *6-1c*
checkout assistant Kassiererin *11-3a T*
chemistry Chemie *1-3d*
childhood Kindheit *3-4d T*
Chrismas Eve Heiligabend *5-3a EP*
chum Kumpel *2-3b*
citizen Bürger(in) *5-6a*
civilization Zivilisation *7-4c T*
classmate Klassenkamerad(in) *2-3b*
climate Klima *6-4b*
(be) close to someone jemandem nahe (sein) *2-3b*
cloth Stoff *12-1d*
clumsy ungeschickt *10-2d*
collapse zusammenbrechen *3-4b*
commitment Verpflichtung *6-3c*
community service gemeinnützige Arbeit *5-4e*
companion Gefährte (Gefährtin) *2-3b*
company outing Betriebsausflug *11-1b*
compared to verglichen mit *6-2c*
competitor Mitbewerber(in) *2-2e EP*
complain sich beschweren *5-3a*
concept Konzept *6-4b*
condition Zustand *4-6d*
conditions of life Lebensumstände *3-1d*
confusion Verwirrung *10-3c*
connected to verbunden sein mit *2-3d T*
constantly ständig *8-1b*
context Zusammenhang *9-3d*
convenient bequem *6-1b T*
cooker Kocher *7-4a*
copy abschreiben *5-1a*
coral reef Korallenriff *8-3c T*
Cosplay Cosplay *9-3d*
costume Kostüm *9-3d*
cosy Tee- / Eierwärmer *9-2b T*
courgette Zucchini *6-1b T*
create erzeugen *7-4c T*
crime Kriminalität *5*
crocus Krokus *3-3a*
crops Feldfrüchte *7-2a*
crow krähen *6-4d*
crowd Menge *8-1b*
cuddly knuddelig *7-5 EP*
cultivate anbauen *6-4b*
cultural context kultureller Zusammenhang *9-3d*
curl Locke *3-4a*
customize nach Kundenwünschen anfertigen *6-3b*

D

damage zerstören *2-3d T*
(the) Danish die Dänen *3-2d*
dart Pfeil *7-2c*
date of birth Geburtsdatum *2-1a*
deal with zurechtkommen mit *1-2a T*
decimal point Dezimalpunkt *4-2a*
deckchair Liegestuhl *8-3c T*
define definieren *7-1a*
definitely sicher *7-4f T*
delay Verzögerung *11-3a EP*
deliver liefern *6-3c*
delivery Lieferung *6-3c*
delivery conditions Lieferbedingungen *6-3c*
(in) demand (nach)gefragt *1-3d*
Denmark Dänemark *3-2b*
depend abhängen *4-2d*
depressing deprimierend *9-2b T*
derelict verlassen *9-2b T*
description Beschreibung *2-2a*
desperate verzweifelt *6-4d*
despite trotz *2-2b EP*
developing country Entwicklungsland *12-1d*
device Gerät *12-1c*
dialect Dialekt *7-3a*
difference Unterschied *5-4b*
disadvantage Nachteil *3-2c*

disagree anderer Meinung sein *3-1d*
disconnected getrennt, abgeschnitten; hier: ohne Telefon- und Internetverbindung *8*
dish Gericht *3-2b*
dishonest unehrlich *5-1e T*
divided geteilt *7-2c*
diving tauchen *8-3c T*
divorce Scheidung *2-2c*
divorced geschieden *2-1b*
due to aufgrund *2-2e EP*

E

economical ökonomisch *6-4b*
electrical power Strom *7-4a*
emergency Notfall *7-4f T*
(be) employed eine Festanstellung haben *10-1d*
employee Angestellte(r) *1-3d*
enable befähigen *9-3d*
enchanting bezaubernd *8-5 EP*
encourage ermuntern *5-1e T*
endangered gefährdet *8-1a*
energy Energie *7-4a*
engaged verlobt *12-2b*
enjoyable angenehm *10-1a*
enjoyment Vergnügen *3-2a*
enormous riesig *3-4d T*
environmental Umwelt- *6-4b*
escalation Eskalation *2-4a*
especially besonders *6-1b T*
eternal ewig *3-4b*
even though obwohl *2-3d T*
everlasting immerwährend *3-4a*
exaggerate übertreiben *8-1b*
excellent ausgezeichnet *3-2c*
exception Ausnahme *2-2c EP*
exclude ausschließen *6-3c*
excursion Ausflug *8-5 EP*
expect to erwarten *3-2a*

F

fail durchfallen *5-1e T*
far away weit entfernt *7-4f T*
fare-dodging schwarzfahren *5-1c*
farming Anbau *6-4a*
feature Programmpunkt *4-5c T*
(be) fed up with something etwas satt haben *2-4a*
feeling Gefühl *1-2a T*
female weiblich *2-1a*
fertilizer Dünger *6-3b*
finally schließlich *7-4f T*
few wenig *5-5c*
financial security finanzielle Sicherheit *3-4d T*
fine Geldstrafe *5-2b*
(I'm) fine mir geht's gut *9-2a T*
Finland Finnland *3-2a*
firm fest *2-3e*
fish dish Fischgericht *3-2b*
flooding Flut *2-2e EP*
fluent fließend *1-2e*
followed by gefolgt von *3-2a*
(by) force (mit) Gewalt *5-4c*
freelance Freiberufler *2-1a*
freeze einfrieren *4-5c T*
freezer Gefriergerät *4-5c T*
freight ship Frachtschiff *6-2a T*
fuel Brennstoff *6-2a T*
full stop Punkt (Satzzeichen) *4-2a*
further weiter *6-4d*
furious wütend *6-2b*

G

galaxy Galaxie *8-1a*
garbage Müll *2-3d T*
gardening Gartenarbeit *4-5c T*
garlic Knoblauch *6-1b T*
gather sammeln *7-2c*
gender Geschlecht *2-1a*
(in) general im allgemeinen *5-5c*
genetic manipulation Genmanipulation *6-3b*
genset Generator *7-4c T*
gentle sanft *8-1 EP*
geocaching Geocaching (eine Art Schnitzeljagd mit GPS) *9-3d*
giant riesig *5-3a EP*
glance at einen Blick auf etw. werfen *6-1b T*
go on fortsetzen *3-2c*
go public an die Börse gehen *2-3d T*
GPS receiver GPS Empfänger *9-3d*
graphic designer Grafikdesigner(in) *2-4a*
grid Stromnetz *7-4f T*
groundhopping Stadion-Hüpfen *9-3d*
grow anbauen *4-5a*
growing number wachsende Zahl *8-1b*
growth Wachstum *9-3d*
guaranteed garantiert *6-3c*
guerrilla Guerilla- *9-2a T*

H

hang out rumhängen *2-3d T*
happiness Glück *3*
hatred Hass *2-4a*
head of facilities Gebäudemanager *11-3a T*
head of marketing Marketingleiter *2-1a*
healthy gesund *6-3b*
(in) heaven's name um Himmels willen *6-2a T*
herd Herde *2-3d T*
hidden versteckt *9-3h*
hide and seek Versteck spielen *9-3d*
hijacking Entführung *5-4a*
Hindi Hindi, Amtssprache in Indien *1-2a T*
(be) homesick Heimweh (haben) *3-4d T*

host family Gastfamilie *1-3d*
hot-air balloon Heißluftballon *7-6 EP*
hotel resort Hotelanlage *8-1a*
huge riesig *7-3 EP*
Hungarian Ungar(in) *1-2a*
Hungary Ungarn *1-2a T*
hunter Jäger *7-3a*
hunting Jagd *7-2a*
hustle and bustle Hektik *8-1b*

I

ideal ideal *3-1d*
idiom Redewendung *10-3c*
illegal illegal *5-6a*
including einschließlich *6-2a T*
incoming eingehend *8-3c T*
increasingly mehr und mehr *6-3b*
independence Unabhängigkeit *1-3d*
Indian Inder(in) *1-2a*
informal informell *2-3b*
ingredient Zutat *6-3b*
inherit erben *10-1b T*
innocent unschuldig *2-4a*
inquiry Anfrage *1-3d*
insist on bestehen auf *8-1b*
inspiration Inspiration *8-1e*
interact interagieren *9-3d*
interest Interesse *2-1a*
Internet access Internetzugang *8-1a*
Internet connection Internet-Verbindung *8-1b*
internship Praktikum *12-3a T*
interpreting Dolmetschen *10-3e*
involve beinhalten *9-3d*
Iranian Iraner(in) *2-4a*
ironic ironisch *2-2e EP*
island Insel *5-5c*
Israeli Israeli *2-4a*
item Artikel *6-3c*

J

Japanese Japaner(in) *3-4d T*
jay-walking regelwidriges Überqueren einer Straße *5-1c*
jewel Juwel *4-4c*
job application Stellenbewerbung *11-2a*
join sich anschließen *6-3b*
judge Richter *5-2b*
jug Kännchen *9-3b*
jungle Dschungel *7-3c*

K

keen on etwas sehr gerne tun *4-5c T*
(you're) kidding! das ist doch nicht dein Ernst! *8-3c T*
knit stricken *1-4a EP*
kph Kilometer pro Stunde *5-5c*

L

label Etikett *6-1b T*
lamp post Straßenlaterne *3-4b*
landscape designer Landschafts-architekt *6-4b*
large groß *2-2a*
lately kürzlich *6-1b T*
lawn Rasen *5-3a*
lead führen *3-2a*
league Liga *9-3d*
leak undicht sein *9-4 EP*
legal gesetzlich *9-2b T*
legal permission gesetzliche Genehmigung *6-4d*
lend jemandem etw. leihen *4-1*
live in harmony with in Einklang leben mit *6-4b*
loads of Mengen von *8-1b*
loan Darlehen *4-4a*
local Einheimische(r) *2-2d EP*
local örtlich *3-4d T*
local farmer ein Bauer vor Ort *6-1c*
local product Produkt aus der Gegend *6-2c*
locally grown vor Ort angebaut *6-1c*
lock Schloss *3-4a*
locked in eingeschlossen in *3-4b*
logbook Logbuch *9-3d*
long haul flight Langstrecken-Flug *11-3a T*
look forward to sich freuen auf *1-2a T*
(the) lot alles *6-1b T*
love padlock Liebesschloss *3-4a*
lovely hübsch *9-3b*
lyrics Liedtext *1-2a T*

M

magic magisch *3-4a*
maid Zimmermädchen *10-1b T*
magnificent großartig *8-5 EP*
marriage Ehe *2-2c*
massive enorm *9-3d*
mattress Matratze *4-3b*
mayor Bürgermeister *9-2b T*
meaningful bedeutungsvoll *8-1b*
means of transport Transport-mittel *6-1a*
(be) meant to soll *9-2d*
member Mitglied *6-3b*
midday Mittagszeit *5-2a*
milk jug Milchkännchen *9-3b*
mobile phone Handy *8-1a*
monk Mönch *8-1b*
mother tongue Muttersprache *10-3b*
mother-in-law Schwiegermutter *2-2a*
motor racing Autorennen *5-5c*
motorway Autobahn *5-5c*
mouth-watering appetitlich *6-3c*
movement Bewegung *9-2d*
mow mähen *5-3a*
mph Meilen pro Stunde *5-5c*
mugger Straßenräuber *5-4d*
mugging Straßenraub *5-4a*

N

need Bedürfnis *6-3b*
negotiation Verhandlung *10-3e*
neither ... nor weder ... noch *3-1d*
nephew Neffe *2-2a*
(the) Netherlands die Niederlande *3-2a*
New Zealander Neuseeländer *3-1b*
niece Nichte *2-2a*
nightmare Albtraum *8-3c T*
nomadic nomadisch *7-2c*
North Cape Nordkap *1-4a EP*
Norway Norwegen *1-4a EP*
not quite nicht ganz *9-2b T*
notice wahrnehmen *3-4b*
nowadays heutzutage *12-1c*
nun Nonne *8-1b*
nutrient rich nahrhaft *6-3b*

O

organic food Bionahrung *6-3b*
organic produce Bioprodukt *6-3c*
organically grown biologisch angebaut *12-3a T*
orienteering Orientierungslauf *9-3d*
originate den Ursprung haben *9-3d*
outgoing abgehend *8-3c T*
outing Ausflug *11-1b*
Oxfam shop Dritte-Welt-Laden *3-4d T*

P

paddle paddeln *7-4f T*
pal Kumpel *2-3b*
participant Teilnehmer *9-3d*
pass on weiterleiten *12-1d*
patchwork Patchwork *2-2b*
pay rise Gehaltserhöhung *11-4a*
pear Birne *6-1a*
performance art Kunstdarbietung *9-3d*
permanent job Festanstellung *10-1c*
permission Genehmigung *6-4d*
personal persönlich *1-1b*
personal information persönliche Angaben *2-1b*
pesticide Pestizid *6-3b*
phenomenon Phänomen *9-3d*
phone in sick sich telefonisch krank melden *5-1a*
pick pocketing Taschendiebstahl *5-4a*
pick up aufheben *2-2e EP*
pick up somebody jemanden abholen *1-3d*
pigeon Taube *8-2a*
piracy Piraterie *5-1c*
planet Planet *8-3c T*
plant Pflanze *6-4b*
plant-based auf pflanzlicher Basis *7-2c*
pleasant nett *10-1a*
plenty of time viel Zeit *4-5c T*
poison Gift *7-2c*
politician Politiker *2-4a*
popular beliebt *6-3c*
popular culture Popkultur *9-3d*
populous bevölkerungsreich *8-5 EP*
position berufliche Position *1-3d*
post something etwas posten *2-3d T*
pouch Beutel *7-3 EP*
precisely genau *8-1b*
pressure Druck *5-1e T*
Prince Charming Märchenprinz *2-2b EP*
printer paper Druckerpapier *5-1a*
privacy settings persönliche Sicherheitseinstellungen *2-3d T*
probation Bewährung *5-4e*
produce Produkt *6-3c*
professional league Fußball Bundes- und Regionalliga *9-3d*
property Eigentum *5-4c*
proverb Sprichwort *10-3c*
provide liefern *8-1b*
(go) public an die Börse gehen *2-3d T*
public transport öffentlicher Verkehr *3-2c*
(be) published veröffentlicht (werden) *3-4b*
publisher Verleger *11-3a EP*
pumpkin Kürbis *6-4d*
(be) punished bestraft (werden) *5-1e T*
punishment Strafe 5
purpose Sinn *10-1a*

Q

(not) quite (nicht) ganz *9-2b T*
quite a few ziemlich viele *7-4c T*

R

railing Geländer *9-2b T*
rainforest Regenwald *7-2a*
receive empfangen *6-3c*
receiver Empfänger *9-3d*
recently kürzlich *5-5c*
reduced herabgesetzt *5-5c*
reef Riff *8-3c T*
regardless of ungeachtet *9-3d*
regatta Regatta *2-2e EP*
registered angemeldet *1-3d*
regular regelmässig *6-3c*
regular supply regelmässige Versorgung *7-4c T*
related verwandt *7-2a*
relationship Beziehung *2-3d T*
reliable zuverlässig *1-3d*
rely on abhängig von *7-2c*
remote entlegen *5-3a EP*
remove entfernen *3-4b*
repeat wiederholen *7-4e*

report berichten *3-2a*
represent vertreten *4-4a*
require benötigen *11-2a*
rescue retten *8-1b*
respect Respekt *2-2c*
responsible verantwortlich *1-1d*
retire in den Ruhestand gehen *1-4b*
retired im Ruhestand *2-1a*
retirement Ruhestand *12-4a*
(in) return for dafür *4-4c*
reverse umkehren *8-1b*
ride Fahrt *5-2b*
riverbed Flußbett *2-2e EP*
robbery Raub *5-4a*
room and board Unterkunft und Verpflegung *1-3d*
room maid Zimmermädchen *10-1b T*
rooster Hahn *6-4d*
run betreiben *7-1 EP*
run-down runtergekommen *9-2c*
runny nose laufende Nase *11-3a EP*
rural ländlich *8-1b*

S

sadness Traurigkeit *3-2a*
sanity Gesundheit *8-1b*
Santa Claus Weihnachtsmann *1-4a EP*
(be) satisfied with zufrieden (sein) mit *3-1d*
satnav Navi *11-3c*
savings Ersparnisse *4-3b*
saying Redensart *10-3c*
(be) scared Angst haben *11-3a T*
scenery Landschaft *3-1b*
school-leaver Schulabgänger *3-2c*
security Sicherheit *4-4a*
seeing someone mit jemandem zusammen sein *2-1b*
self-employed selbstständig *12-1d*
selfish eigennützig *8-1b*
sense Sinn *2-4a*
service something etwas überholen *9-4 EP*
several times mehrere Male *7-3c*
sew nähen *12-2a T*
(be) shaped like geformt (sein) wie *9-3b*
share teilen *7-2a*
sheep Schaf *2-3d T*
sheet Zettel, Blatt *5-1e T*
shoplifter Ladendieb *5-4d*
shoplifting Ladendiebstahl *5-4a*
shopping trolley Einkaufswagen *5-2a*
short for kurz für *9-3d*
shortage Knappheit *7-4f T*
shortly after kurz nach *3-4b*
shotgun Schrotflinte *7-2c*
show up hingehen *2-4a*
shy schüchtern *1-2a T*
sick krank *5-1a*
(do a) sickie „krank machen" *5-1a*
silver brooch Silberbrosche *9-3b*
similar ähnlich *11-4b T*
site Website *2-3d T*
skill Fähigkeit *8-1e*
skip Müllcontainer *4-5c T*
skyscraper Wolkenkratzer *6-4d*
slightly ein wenig *3-1d*
smoke signal Rauchzeichen *8-2a*
social security soziale Sicherheit *3-2d*
solar Solar *7-4a*
solution Lösung *7-4f T*
source Quelle *9-3d*
space Platz *6-4d*
(in) space im Weltraum *8-1a*
span Umfang, Dauer *8-1b*
spare key Ersatzschlüssel *9-4 EP*
spear Speer *7-2c*
specific spezifisch *9-3d*
spectator Zuschauer *2-2e EP*
speed limit Geschwindigkeitsbegrenzung *5-5b*
speeding Überschreiten der Geschwindigkeit *12-4a*
stadium Stadion *9-3d*
statistics Statistik *3-2c*
status Familienstand *2-1a*
stepmother Stiefmutter *2-2a*
stepson Stiefsohn *2-2c*
strange seltsam *6-1b T*
study Studie *3-2a*
stuff Zeug *6-1b T*
subculture Subkultur *9-3d*
substance Substanz *7-1 EP*
suit passen *11-3a*
supply Versorgung *7-4c T*
supporter Fan *9-3d*
suppose annehmen *2-2c EP*
surrounded by umgeben von *7-1 EP*
survey Umfrage *4-3b*
swear schwören *3-4b*
switch off ausschalten *7-5c*

T

table mat Tisch Set *9-3b*
take part teilnehmen *3-2a*
take place stattfinden *4-3b*
tasty schmackhaft *6-2a T*
temporary grandma Großmutter auf Zeit *1-3d*
temporary job Zeitarbeit *10-1c*
term Begriff *9-2d*
territory Gebiet *7-2a*
text eine SMS schreiben *8-3c T*
text message SMS
tidy aufräumen *10-2b*
tie Krawatte *9-3d*
tipped with eingetaucht in *7-2c*
top spot erste Stelle *3-2a*
topic Thema *3-4d T*
(in) touch in Verbindung *2-3d T*

toy with spielen mit *2-2b EP*
traffic conditions Verkehrsbedingungen *5-5c*
treasure Schatz *9-3h*
treasure-hunting Schatzsuche *9-3d*
tribe Stamm *7-2a*
trigger auslösen *2-4a*
trolley Wagen, Karren *5-2a*
tropical tropisch *7-2a*
trusted vertrauenswürdig *6-3b*
(your) turn Sie sind an der Reihe *3-4d T*
turn out to be sich herausstellen, dass *1-4a EP*

U

unconventional unkonventionell *8-1b*
unfortunately leider *5-2b*
unplugged unplugged („ausgesteckt", „ohne Strom") *8-1b*
unusual ungewöhnlich *7-3a*
upset verärgern *12-3a T*
urban städtisch *8-1 EP*
use Verwendung *9-3d*

V

vacant offen *11-2a*
valuable wertvoll *2-2b*
value Wert *4-4c*
vandalism Vandalismus *5-4a*
variety Vielfalt *3-2d*
venue Veranstaltungsort *9-3d*
vertical vertikal *6-4a*
viable machbar *6-4b*
view Blick *9-2b T*
virus (Computer)virus *2-3d T*
vital sehr wichtig *8-1b*
volcano Vulkan *5-3a EP*
voluntary work ehrenamtliche Tätigkeit *3-4d T*

W

wardrobe Kleiderschrank *4-3b*
waste Verschwendung *2-3d T*
wasted verschwendet *4-5c T*
wear tragen *5-5b*
weight Gewicht *3-4b*
(be) well off reich (sein) *5-3a EP*
whenever jedes Mal, wenn *7-5c*
wide groß *3-2d*
wonder sich fragen *3-4b*
workload Arbeitsbelastung *5-1e T*
world-famous weltberühmt *8-1b*
(be) worth wert (sein) *2-3d T*

Classroom language

Understanding the teacher
Turn to page …
Walk about and talk to other people.
Work in pairs.
Find a partner to work with
Get into (new) groups of three or four.
Take turns to ask and answer.
Choose the most interesting questions.
Report back to the class on your discussion.
Read the article …
Match the words to the definitions.
Tick the correct answer.
Listen to the recording.
Look at the pictures on page …

Talking to the teacher
What page are we on?
What do we have to do for homework?
What should we do for the next lesson?
Can you write that on the board, please?
What is … in English?
How can I say … in English?
What should we do now?
Should we make new groups?

Talking to a partner / to others
Do you want to work with me?
Can I interview you / ask you some questions?
What have you written?
Have you got any ideas?
Can you guess my words?
What advantages / disadvantages / pros / cons can you think of?

Asking what others think
What's your opinion?
What do you think?
Do you agree?
Which questions do you find most interesting?
Which is the best / funniest / most interesting …?

Making suggestions
Let's make a list.
Let's work together.
Let's ask …
Why don't we write some questions?
Let's swap with …

Finding out
What questions can you think of?
What questions / information have you got?
Can you tell me your answers?
What did you guess?
Have you got the same as me?
What does this mean?
Have you done the homework?
Have you finished reading the text?
Can you answer all the questions?
Why are you in this course?
What do you want to improve?
What do you need English for?

Working in a group
We've now got five minutes to do this.
Let's do it like this.
Who wants to write this?
We have to collect as many ideas as possible / prepare a presentation / ask other people …
Who's going to report back to the class?

Reporting to the class
What surprised us most was …
We all think …
Most people in the class think …
We won the game!
We know the most words!
We got all the answers right!
The most interesting bit of information is …

List of references

Page 7: © Thinkstock/iStockphoto
Page 8: © Thinkstock/Photodisc/Michael Blann
Page 9: from left © iStockphoto/Stalman;
© Thinkstock/iStockphoto; © iStockphoto/Claudiad
Page 10: Photo © Thinkstock/Comstock; Text adapted from
© Goethe-Institut e. V., Internet-Redaktion March 2012
Page 12: top © fotolia/Benicce; Mitte © Thinkstock/iStockphoto;
bottom© Thinkstock/iStockphoto
Page 13: © Thinkstock/iStockphoto
Page 14: © iStockphoto/bonniej
Page 15: poster with kind permission of© Ronny Edry,
Peace Factory www.israelovesiran.com
Page 16: © Thinkstock/iStockphoto
Page 17: © imago/PanoramiC
Page 18: © iStockphoto/mikeuk
Page 19: © Glow Images/ChameleonsEyeRF
Page 20: © Thinkstock/iStockphoto
Page 21: © Thinkstock/iStockphoto
Page 23: © Copyright 2013 Henley on Todd Inc. All Rights
Reserved. www.henleyontodd.com.au, Alice Springs
Page 26: © Thinkstock/iStockphoto
Page 27: both photos © Thinkstock/iStockphoto
Page 29: © iStockphoto/whitemay
Page 30: © iStockphoto/KirbusEdvard
Page 31: © Thinkstock/iStockphoto
Page 32: © fotolia/Grecaud Paul
Page 34: © iStockphoto/CEFutcher
Page 35: © Thinkstock/Stockbyte/George Doyle
Page 36: both photos © Thinkstock/iStockphoto
Page 37: © Thinkstock/Comstock
Page 38: © Thinkstock/iStockphoto
Page 40: top © Thinkstock/iStockphoto;
bottom © Glow Images/Iconotec
Page 41: © epd-bild/Rolf Zoellner
Page 42: © iStockphoto/bowdenimages
Page 43: Illustrations © iStockphoto/-Mosquito-
Page 45: © Thinkstock/iStockphoto
Page 47: from top © Thinkstock/iStockphoto;
© fotolia/arekmalang; © iStockphoto/lostinbids;
© fotolia/andrea lehmkuhl; © Thinkstock/iStockphoto
Page 48: from top © Thinkstock/Stockbyte;
© Thinkstock/iStockphoto (2x);
© Thinkstock/ Brand X Pictures/Jupiterimages
Page 49: top © Thinkstock/iStockphoto;
bottom © fotolia/Robert Kneschke
Page 51: © iStockphoto/anouchka
Page 52: top © fotolia/maximino gomes;
bottom © fotolia/Roman Shiyanov
Page 53: © Thinkstock/iStockphoto
Page 54: top © iStockphoto/londoneye;
bottom © iStockphoto/JohnnyLye
Page 55: © Klaus Richter
Page 56: top © Thinkstock/iStockphoto;
bottom © iStockphoto/EdStock
Page 58: a © iStockphoto/asbe; b © iStockphoto/Lepro ;
c © iStockphoto/VMJones; d © iStockphoto/vecstar ;
e © iStockphoto/FrankvandenBergh;
f © iStockphoto/pictafolio
Page 59: © Thinkstock/iStockphoto
Page 60: top© iStockphoto/lorenzo104;
bottom © Thinkstock/Hemera
Page 61: © ddp images/dapd
Page 62: top © iStockphoto/Rebekkah_ann;
bottom © PantherMedia/Vichaya Kiatying-Angsulee
Page 63: The Groundspeak Geocaching Logo is a registered
trademark of Groundspeak, Inc. Used with permission (http://
www.groundspeak.com). Texts on Geocaching and Cosplay
adapted from en.wikipedia.org; Foto Cosplay
© iStockphoto/NNehring
Page 64: © iStockphoto/kerriekerr
Page 67: © Thinkstock/iStockphoto
Page 69: © Thinkstock/iStockphoto
Page 70: © Thinkstock/Getty Images/Jupiterimages
Page 71: © Thinkstock/iStockphoto
Page 73: © Thinkstock/iStockphoto
Page 74: from left © Thinkstock/Monkey Business;
© Thinkstock/Goodshoot; © Thinkstock/Comstock (2x)
Page 75: © fotolia/goodluz
Page 76: © Thinkstock/iStockphoto
Page 78: from top © fotolia/Alterfalter;
© Thinkstock/iStockphoto; © fotolia/Yuri Arcurs
Page 79: © fotolia/Daniel Tackley
Page 80: © iStockphoto/kupicoo
Page 81: © Thinkstock/iStockphoto
Page 82: Tweet © iStockphoto/kizilkayaphotos;
thief © iStockphoto/Double_Vision;
plants © mauritius/Alamy;
man © Thinkstock/iStockphoto
Page 84: top© Thinkstock/iStockphoto;
bottom© iStockphoto/nycshooter
Page 85: © iStockphoto/stevecoleimages
Page 87: © fotolia/Michael Fritzen
Page 88: © iStockphoto/Yurilux
Page 92: © iStockphoto/Photomorphic
Page 93: © Thinkstock/iStockphoto
Page 95 and 96: © fotolia/Roman Shiyanov